ESTIMONIALS

*Responses from friends who read an early edition of
this book, some of whom appear in our story.*

A wonderful tribute to Sandy . . . to love . . . to fighting
with all one's might! How bravely you and Sandy went
through your battle not only with cancer but with the
medical profession as well. . . . It is a beautiful book,
Art. Thank you for writing it. As so many friends have
said, you have a wonderful way with words and your
sense of humor is such a joy.

> —*Nancy & Bill Hunt, friends
> and fellow travelers on our Around the World trip*

Thank you for not being afraid to share with the world
your intense love for a woman that deserved your love,
for touching my husband's heart the way you did with
writing the book, for inspiring us all to love our partners each and every day because you know firsthand
too well how short that time can be.

> —*Debbie Muller, who directed us to the doctor in the
> Dominican Republic, leading to the cancer center in Mississippi,
> which, I believe, gave me and Sandy a few more months together.*

You have a gift that makes it easy for anyone to understand your writing . . . Your book will be an inspiration to me and others who will have to face the tough
choices and find the courage to fight on, and I want to
thank you for bearing your soul and writing this.

> —*Ralph Muller, Debbie's husband—our friends
> from the Mountain*

Too many people, good people, never know a love such as yours. From your words and those of your children and friends, Sandy was certainly a very special lady . . . Her struggle was heartbreaking to read. I can only imagine the words and thought that were not put to pen and paper . . . It is truly a labor of love and your love shines throughout these pages in between the pain of losing her.

—Iris Fagin, a friend since high school

As I began to read the book I could not put it down. Your words of love for Sandy, and even your way of expressing your heart with others, such an inspiration. So many never find a love like you and Sandy had. . .The memories can bring zest and vitality back into your life.

—Sallie Vander Ploeg, an acquaintance from the Mountain

Having known & loved Sandy, it was a tear jerker just remembering all her ups and downs, yet she was still able to smile with us.

—Shelby & Doug Pilkington, our first friends on the Mountain

After having read (many times) your glorious tale of life, death, and love, I must tell you how proud I am of you and Sandy and all that you achieved and shared. My dearest cousin/friend/brother, across all our years, now and forever I love and admire you.

—My cousin Audrey, the older sister I never had

An inspiring story of love, friendship, understanding, commitment, faith and an unyielding effort to overcome in the face of insurmountable odds.

—Bobby Ciovacco, my friend since we shared a fire escape in childhood, and today my trusted lawyer.

CHAMPAGNE
AND
ROSES

CHAMPAGNE
AND
ROSES

A Story of Love and Cancer

ARTHUR J. BENSON

 VANTAGEPress

Cover design by Pauline Neuwirth, Neuwirth & Associates
Vantage Press and the Vantage Press colophon
are registered trademarks of Vantage Press, Inc.

FIRST EDITION
Published by Vantage Press, Inc.
419 Park Ave. South, New York, NY 10016

Photo on page 5 of photo section by Jeff Walling, sitting #15-0024 © Club
Services of America, 406 S. Rockford Drive, Suite 6, Tempe AZ 85281.
Used with permission.

Manufactured in the United States of America
ISBN: 978-0-533-16417-2

Library of Congress Catalog Card No: 2010913272

0 9 8 7 6 5 4 3 2

For Sandy, who taught me how to love,
and because of her, I can love again.

Contents

Introduction
1

CHAMPAGNE
AND
ROSES

Introduction

THIS BOOK IS the story of the twenty-one months my wife, Sandy, had cancer. It concerns the time from her diagnosis on June 23, 2005, until her death on the morning of March 15, 2007, at the age of sixty-six. During this long and difficult struggle, I had kept our numerous friends around the country and the world updated by e-mail. After it was all over, I was urged over and over to write a book in the hope that others going through the same thing would not feel so alone and that people could learn something about managing their medical options and know what to insist on. I will always believe that what we finally learned in Mississippi, a mere four months before Sandy died, could have if not saved her life, certainly extended it indefinitely. If we had learned about this rather simple and entirely logical procedure in the beginning, she might be alive and cancer-free today. Here is Sandy's story.

Chapter 1
About Sandy, About Us

SANDRA SUE SNYDER was born on June 16, 1940, in Nix Hospital in San Antonio, Texas. For those of you who have been to San Antonio and taken the Riverwalk boat tour, Nix Hospital is the building that looks like a single wall facade. A wonderful optical illusion. It's fitting that Sandy was born there because she was like an optical illusion in so many ways—a joyous wonder who brought sunshine into the lives of all she touched.

Her parents, Justin and Ida Mae Snyder, took her back to their home in Aransas Pass, Texas, when she was a few days old. Sandy was a Houston on her mother's side (a pretty well known name in Texas) and one-quarter Cherokee Indian on her father's side. She was an only child. She had a wholesome life growing up in Aransas Pass, which is on the Gulf Coast in an area called the Coastal Bend. It is a fishing and tourist area about twenty miles north of Corpus Christi. Sandy attended Aransas Pass High School, where aside from being an A student and majorette, she was voted the most beautiful girl in her senior class of 1958. There were sixty-two students in her graduating class. The town was slightly smaller than Texas hair. Sandy was all set to go to Southern Methodist University, and even had a roommate assigned, when a customer walked into her daddy's Pontiac dealership, saw a picture of her in her majorette outfit, and asked if she had a scholarship for baton twirling. When her daddy told him that she didn't, the man said he knew of a school where she might get one. Next thing she knew, she was on a plane heading for an audition at the University of Miami in Florida. The audition must have gone well because she was offered a full scholarship. I always kidded her about it. She majored in foreign languages and was a straight-A student. She later taught French and Spanish on the high school level, and earned a master's degree in education, as well as a paralegal degree. Yet with all those great academic credentials that she would acquire she went to college on a full scholarship for baton twirling—go figure!

A little-known and rather ironic fact is that the United States was the first country to recognize Fidel Castro's regime in Cuba. In fact, we sent the University of Miami Hurricane Band to Cuba to perform for Castro. Sandy, of course, was part of that as a Majorette. As she told the story, they went to Cuba aboard 1939 Cuban Air Force DC 3's, reliable, but old aircraft. The planes had no plexiglass in the windows and everyone was seated along the cabin facing each other on long strips of canvas. They were told to hold their luggage between their knees for takeoff and landing. Unfortunately, when they started their takeoff roll, much of the luggage came loose and rolled to the back of the aircraft, preventing a takeoff, so they tried it again, this time successfully. When they finally got to Havana they were quartered in the Havana Hilton which, Sandy said, was pock-marked by bullet holes and had been trashed.

Sandy was in a room on the fifth floor. The next day,

when they were to perform for Castro, Sandy got in the elevator in her little Majorette outfit and pressed *Lobby*. The elevator stopped on the fourth floor and four bearded guerillas got on, wearing fatigues with ammunition bandoliers across their chests. She tried to shrink into a corner and came close to panic when the elevator skipped the lobby floor and went directly to the basement. She thought for sure she was dead. Instead they all got off and she went back up to the lobby, still scared to death. The Hurricane Band did the performance and then went out to the airport for the flight back to Miami. Unfortunately, the Cuban pilots showed up drunk, so the band was obliged to spend the night on the terminal floor before getting back to Miami the next day. Sandy said that if her parents had ever found out they'd have had a fit. I would imagine so.

While at the University of Miami, Sandy met a boy from New York, and they were married after graduating in 1962. While he went to dental school in Baltimore, she was a teacher. She continued teaching in Wichita Falls, Texas, where he was stationed as a dentist at Shepard Air Force Base. She then moved with him to Westchester County, New York, where he set up a practice in Yonkers. They had a son, Alan Girard, Jr., and Sandy eventually went into the real estate business. The marriage ended in a divorce after twenty-one years.

My full name is Arthur Jay Benson. I grew up in New York in the area of the South Bronx known as Fort Apache, named for the 41st Police Precinct house. I always said that I was the least favorite of my father's children. The thing that made that particularly annoying was that, like Sandy, I too was an only child.

I went to P.S. 48 in the Bronx, the same grammar school my parents attended. From there I went to Morris High School. Colin Powell was a senior there when I was a freshman. In my mid-teens, my parents and I moved to Queens. I actually had my own room instead of sleeping on the couch in the living room. It was a great thrill. I transferred to Jamaica High School and then to Martin Van Buren High School, where I was part of the first graduating class. I went to college at Adelphi University in Garden City, New York, and graduated in 1962.

I began my professional career working for a retail chain, then served several years in the U.S. Air Force, which I left as a Captain in 1967. From there, two partners and I borrowed a desk and a telephone in a lawyer's office in lower Manhattan, five blocks from where they were building the World Trade Center, and set up a national service business called Sure Air Ltd. After twelve years of working 365 days a year we were an "overnight success." Of course, in the New York tradition, as soon as we got successful I had to have the other guys whacked. Just kidding!

During this time, I was married approximately six years each to Alexis Benson, whom I met in college and who gave me two wonderful sons, Matthew and Mark, and to the now Daisy Ryan, who blessed me with Leah, the sunshine of my life. I used to joke that there was a bumper sticker in New York that said, "Honk if you've been married to Arty." Sandy would say that when they all were stopped at the same traffic light, the resulting noise was cacophonous.

I met Sandy at 9:30 A.M. on Wednesday, August 18, 1982, in Bedford, New York, where she was a real estate agent. I was considering moving my offices north of Manhattan to either Long Island or Westchester County. My father would sit at home with the *New York Times* Sunday real estate section and call every real estate office listed and leave my name and office phone number. It reached the point where I would tell the people who returned the calls on Monday to just tell me where the property was and I would see it on my own. Sandy was the only one who insisted that she had to show a place personally. I finally said I would meet her on Tuesday, August 17. She said no, her son had an orthodontist appointment. I couldn't believe it. My first thought was, "Lady, you gotta be kidding." She said Wednesday would be okay, and for some unknown reason, I agreed.

That morning I went to meet her at 9:30 A.M. at her office, Ginnel Real Estate. When I walked in, Sandy was working at her desk. Don't ask me how I knew which one of the women there was Sandy; somehow I just knew. She looked up and smiled at me and the rest, as they say, is history. That's why 8/18 became our lucky day. We were married three years later to the day.

I've been asked to describe what was different about my love for Sandy. I can't quite describe it except for a sense that no matter the trials and tribulations, it was right and there was a destiny about it. It was an extremely intense feeling. A physical and emotional longing and a great pride in being around her. I always felt ten feet tall when I walked into a room with her. This book is called *Champagne and Roses* because, from the moment we met, we were blessed to live a "champagne and roses" lifestyle. We enjoyed champagne often, and I would get Sandy a dozen roses at least once a month. At our wedding in Texas, we served nothing but Moet Chandon Brut (we had a second wedding in New York a few months later for the rest of the rabble). I wrote poetry for her several times a year. Sandy was beautiful, outrageous, impulsive, irreverent, flamboyant, and simply took over any room she was in. She had a dazzling smile, always knew exactly how to pose for a camera, and probably loved animals more than people. She always said that the wrong species was on top of the food chain. B.B., our white Whippet (who died at age fifteen on New Year's Eve 2007) was her favorite dog of all time, partially at least because he was a brat. He was the son of Luke, the Whippet who won Best in Show at the prestigious Westminster Kennel Club Dog Show. He always knew he was royalty. We did, however, get him for nothing. He had this little problem. His testicles didn't descend, making him useless as a show dog, as well as other things. I thought it was obvious what his name should be. I named him Highball. Our daughter, Leah, was eleven at the time and didn't get it. She said, "Eyeball, Daddy? What kind of name is Eyeball?" I figured that I wasn't going to explain this, so he became B.B. His full name was H. (for Highball) Bentley Benson (because he was aristocratic) The Only (because there wasn't going to be any more of him). The ashes of both B.B. and our other Whippet, Gabriella, are buried at Sandy's feet.

On Memorial Day weekend, 2005, Sandy and I were elected "Homecoming King and Queen of the Mountain" where we were living in North Carolina, at a wonderful place called Mountain Air, succeeding our dear friends, John and Linda Silvati. I still have the crown and tiara. They will probably not do a homecoming King and Queen again so Sandy and I are King and Queen in perpetuity.

Mountain Air is a flying and golf community on top of a 4,919-foot mountain near the town of Burnsville. Our lives were a fairy tale. It's just that the happily ever after didn't last long enough. I will forever cherish this letter I received from Sandy on our fifteenth wedding anniversary, August 18, 2000.

My Dearest Arthur,

Who could have guessed that we'd be celebrating our fifteenth anniversary on top of a mountain in North Carolina?! We've certainly had a diverse, amazing, wonderful tenure together. What is most amazing and wonderful to me is the feeling I have inside when I'm next to you, see you, or even think of you. You are the most extraordinary person. You're a loving, caring, thoughtful father, friend, and husband. And I don't know how I got so lucky. You've allowed me to grow into the kind of person I've always wanted to be, and to have a life that most people would dream of if they only had enough "dream power." Your sense of humor has carried us through some difficult times and has always been a magnet for me. Your sense of family has become mine as you've been the glue that has held us all together. We're so lucky that our kids love us both as well as each other! I guess what I mainly want to say is "thank you"—for being the man I respect more than anyone, for loving me pretty much unconditionally, and for being the righteous center of my universe. I love you with all my heart.

—Sandy

OUR FIRST HOUSE was in Pound Ridge, New York, in Westchester County. We both loved that house and lived in it for seventeen years, the longest either of us had ever lived in one place. The house was on a dead-end street and backed up to Little Gorge Lake, which is absolutely beautiful. It was a California-style ranch house. We did three major renovations over the years, at one point taking it down to the studs. Sandy had a great talent for design and decoration and people were always comfortable in our homes because we truly made them homes, not just houses. An interesting note is that when Hillary Clinton was First Lady and was looking to establish residence in New York for her run for the Senate, she was interested in buying our house, which was not up for sale. One of the criteria was that the house not be on the open market so the public couldn't know that Mrs. Clinton was interested in it. In any event, for a variety of reasons, we decided not to sell it to the Clintons.

In January 2001, I sold my business, Sure Air Ltd. We had a home in Rockport, Texas, which Sandy had designed and decorated. It was ten miles north of Sandy's childhood home in Aransas Pass. I called it the "Taj M'Benson." It was magnificent and was featured in the Sunday magazine section of the *Corpus Christi Caller Times* on November 23, 1997. It was in an area of Rockport called Harbor Oaks and overlooked a lagoon called Canoe Lake. We also had our home in North Carolina, about thirty miles north of Asheville. We found it when we were driving around North Carolina in November, 1998, and had heard of Mountain Air. We decided to take a look. Sandy got out of the car at the reception center at the bottom of the Mountain and said, "I love it here." I said, "Here you love it? We haven't been up THERE yet."

She said, "Oh yes. I love it here." I said, "OK, here's the checkbook." We bought a piece of land that weekend, a condo the next time we were there, and eventually, in 2001, a house near the top of what we would always call "the Mountain." The Mountain has magnificent 100-mile views and is spectacular in all seasons. It is located at one of only two latitudes in the world that has exactly thirteen weeks of each season. It also has a gorgeous golf course with the first nine holes cut around the runway at the top of the Mountain. Seeing this, we decided to sell the house in New York and split our time between Texas and North Carolina. This was also the time when we started to meet people, many of whom you'll meet in these pages. Many of these people would become the best friends we ever had.

A few years after settling at the Mountain, we were visiting friends in Bonita Springs, Florida, Eddie and Norine Corbo. Sandy—as she always did—went around looking at houses. She looked at a model in Naples, and the next thing I knew I was a Floridian! I must admit, I never thought anything would get Sandy out of Texas, but in March 2005 we moved to Naples. Oddly enough, it was to be the last time that Sandy would ever be in Texas, though we had no way of knowing that at the time.

It was in our new home in early 2005, with the two Whippets and our calico cat named Cleocatra, that we noticed that Sandy had been coughing for some time. We decided to have her checked for allergies, and sure enough, she tested positive to being allergic to cats. And that brings our story to Thursday, June 23, 2005, the first day of a nightmare that I'm still living.

Chapter 2

Finding Out

❧

JUNE 23, 2005

We were fine knowing Sandy had an allergy to cats. It was not as though she was going to give up Cleocatra! Regardless, her cough seemed to be worsening, and I finally insisted she go to the doctor. A chest X-ray revealed that there was something in the upper right lobe of her lung, and the recommendation was that it be examined by a radiologist. Sandy jokingly said, "Maybe it's a hairball."

We went home to await word. Around three that afternoon, Sandy got a phone call from her doctor. After a couple of minutes she turned to me and mouthed "cancer." Right then and there I made a private deal with God. I said, "Me or the dogs for Sandy." (Okay, maybe I didn't say me.) As if that news wasn't bad enough, that night our younger whippet, Gabriella, who was ten years old and not particularly sick, lapsed into a coma and died in Sandy's arms as we were racing to the emergency veterinary clinic in Asheville.

It was certainly not one of our better days, and I don't think God was in on my deal.

The doctor told us the tumor would have to be biopsied. After all, it could very well be benign. It would still need to be removed, but at least it wouldn't be life threatening. On June 30th we drove into Asheville for the biopsy. As we were waiting for the results in the recovery room, the doctor, who had performed the biopsy, walked in and without preamble said, "If you're Christian, pray." It was stunningly stupid and insensitive, and I was not only shocked by his behavior, but by how often insensitivity would be shown by doctors and others over the ensuing twenty-one months. After stumbling over his tongue for a while, he recommended a top oncologist at Duke University Medical Center in Durham, North Carolina. It was about two-hundred miles east of us. We called and were able to secure an appointment for July 12th. Now we had nothing to do but wait.

It didn't seem that things were going our way, though. At Mountain Air on the Fourth of July, we were on our way to a party prior to a fireworks display on the runway at the top of the mountain. Everyone in the community travels around the mountain in golf carts. We were on a severe incline (it is, after all, a mountain) and I had to get out of the cart to get a refilled sand bottle. The cart moved just a fraction, but it was enough to catch my left Achilles tendon. Though I didn't immediately know it, I had severed it. It was quite painful, but we would never miss a party. As the saying goes, "It ain't no party without Arty." Sandy propped me up at the bar and Joanne Boker, our hostess, lent me a cane. It was later during the fireworks that one of the orthopedic surgeons that lives on the mountain, Bob Miller, confirmed that the tendon was totally severed. It took six months on crutches and almost a year and a half of exercises to rehabilitate it. After that night, Sandy and I figured maybe we should paint a red cross on our roof.

JULY 12, 2005

We arrived at our meeting at the Duke University Comprehensive Cancer Center with the oncologist. While we were chatting, Dr. Bob Anderson, a friend and neighbor from the Mountain, and another young surgeon who was with him, came in and looked at Sandy's X-ray. The surgeon said he could operate and that there were "good margins," meaning there was sufficient room all around the tumor to remove it successfully. He thought that he could get the whole tumor by removing the upper right lobe of her lung. He also said that if he couldn't get it all, the whole operation would take less than an hour; if he could get it all, he would, and it would take longer. This seemed to be the path to take. He was free the next afternoon—July 13th at 1:00 P.M.—to operate on Sandy.

On the day of the operation, I will always remember seeing Sandy walking toward the operating room door in a hospital gown and blue hairnet. She looked so tiny and fragile. She stopped and turned back to look at me before the automatic doors closed and I couldn't see her anymore. Our son Alan arrived while she was in the operating room. He had ridden his motorcycle from his home on the Eastern shore of Maryland to be with her.

The operation lasted four hours, so we were very encouraged that everything was being removed. Around 5:00 P.M. the surgeon came out and told us that the operation was a success and he thought he got it all. He had removed the upper lobe of her right lung and a fraction of the middle lobe. The tumor was the size of a large orange and took up two-thirds of the upper lobe. They also removed part of a lymph node to send out for testing. Sandy was prescribed two or three sessions of light chemotherapy to thwart a recurrence. While at Duke, I received a hinged boot for my severed Achilles tendon that I had to wear for the next two or three months, but that was the least of it. Hugely relieved, we spent five days in the hospital in total and left for our home on the mountain on July 17th to resume our lives.

On August 2nd we had dinner on the mountain with Bob Anderson and his wife, Taimi. We had two bottles of champagne to celebrate. On our anniversary, August 18th, we had dinner at one of our favorite restaurants, Gabrielle's at the Richmond Hill Inn in Asheville. We were joined by our very dear friends, John and Linda Silvati, and we stayed overnight since the Richmond Hill Inn was also a lovely bed and breakfast. (It has since burned down.) We continued our celebration of life. Our friend, Norine Corbo, noted, "You don't need a miracle; Sandy's a little miracle all by herself."

What nobody could have known at the time of the operation at Duke was that the cancer had already metastasized to Sandy's spine. Cancer cells travel in the bloodstream and have been likened to grains of sand on a beach that shift with the tide.

Sometime in 2006 Sandy decided to write a book about all of this and call it "Maybe it's a Hairball." I could only find one page, but here it is. This book will finish it for her.

"Maybe it's a Hairball" by Sandra S. Benson

At present I'm sitting in the lap of luxury, I have a wonderful man whom I adore and who loves me more than should be legally allowed.

We have four terrific children and two adorable grandchildren, and life is sooo good. Except. . .

Let me backtrack about a year, and even then you won't understand the scope of our lifestyle and depth of our support group.

In 2005, we made the decision to spend our winters in Naples instead of the Gulf Coast of Texas, which is my home. I say it's my home because, as Texans do, when you're born and reared there, you're always a Texan.

The forty years I spent in Westchester County, N. Y., did wonders for helping me grow up and educating me in the ways of the world. But that entire time was also spent wishing to be back in Texas. My first husband (21 years) had no interest in being west of the Hudson.

My second husband, also a native N. Y.er, did everything he could to see we spent a lot of time there. We always had a place in Tex.

Well, as I mentioned, we gave up our place in Rockport in favor of a grand home in Naples, Florida. It wasn't an easy thing to do, but at the risk of sounding like a snob, we opted for a more upscale lifestyle.

I think she wrote more but this was all I've ever been able to find.

Chapter 3
One Day at a Time

THROUGHOUT SANDY'S AND my twenty-one-month ordeal with her illness, I kept in touch with our family and friends from around the country by sending out periodic e-mail updates. They eventually went to about 150 e-mail addresses in forty-five states. I later found out that they were forwarded and re-forwarded, not only around the United States, but also to other countries as well. This chapter is based on those emails, set mostly in chronological order. They are written by me unless otherwise noted, and contain occasional comments from me. They recount the highs and lows we experienced as one day led to another and we navigated our fate together.

The First Operation at Duke

JULY 20, 2005

We returned from Duke on Sunday evening. They operated on Sandy last Wednesday afternoon. It was a major operation. The main fear was lymph node involvement. They are ninety-nine percent sure they got it all. We will get the results of the micro pathology on the lymph nodes by the end of the week, but they are confident they're clean. Thank you all for your prayers and good vibes, notes, calls, etc. That and an amazing amount of luck really worked.

July 25, 2005

Tomorrow we're off to Duke. A friend is flying us over. Sandy is still quite weak and has a good deal of pain, which is to be expected. We have been unable to find out the results of the micro pathology on her lymph nodes, and have been told that the doctor will tell us tomorrow. Naturally, this is a matter of great concern. We'll update all of you late tomorrow or Wednesday.

July 27, 2005

Here's what happened at Duke: Sandy is healing nicely. Her chest X-ray was clear. We were told the pain and other problems are to be expected. What we didn't know previously was that one lymph node was cancerous and was removed at the same time as the lung lobe. The preliminary results of the micro pathology look fine. The complete results won't be in until tomorrow. They fully expect it to be fine as well. If we don't get a call by the end of the day tomorrow we can assume all is well.

At this point we think we may be able to start to breathe again. She goes back to Duke for her next checkup and to determine the chemo regimen on August 23rd. Thank you all for the myriad of good wishes, the notes, cards, calls, and prayers, and the overwhelming support. So many have done so much we can't begin to repay you. Our love and gratitude to all of you all over the country.

JULY 28, 2005

It's now 7:00 P.M. here, and we've had no calls from the doctors. We were told this means that the micro pathology results were totally negative. We're thrilled, relieved, and emotionally exhausted. We know there's still a bunch of stuff ahead of us (chemo), but it looks like the worst of the nightmare that started a mere four weeks ago today is over. We're not sure whether to laugh, cry, or take a nap. Probably all of the above. Once more, thank you all for everything. You helped make this happen.

JULY 29, 2005

We just got the official phone call: The micro pathology results were negative. And the lymph nodes are clear. Yesterday was five weeks to the day from when this started, not four as I originally miscalculated. Not that it matters. There is no longer any immediate danger. We're all the way out of the woods and out into sunshine. It's pouring here but it's about the prettiest day we've ever seen.

Chemotherapy Begins

OCTOBER 12, 2005

Sandy's first chemo treatment was Monday, and initially she was fine. By yesterday, she was extremely tired, and by last night all her joints ached. The vomiting started at about 6:00 A.M. today. We were told that this was a possibility, but it doesn't make it any easier to go through. For the rest of this week we have to be very careful about infection. Yesterday we went back to Asheville for a shot to boost her white blood cell count. Hopefully this will all pass by the weekend and she'll have two weeks to build herself up for the next round.

As for my Achilles tendon, I finally got rid of the crutches yesterday and am limping around without the brace when I'm on flat, well-lit surfaces. Otherwise, I have to use the brace for another month and have to be careful until at least January. Other than that, everything is terrific. As always, we appreciate your concern. Sandy sends her love to all of you (or would if she weren't napping and knew I was writing this).

OCTOBER 29, 2005

As most of you know, the next chemo treatment is Monday and after that is packing for the trip south to our home in Naples, Florida, and then the actual moving. I will leave N.C. on the 7th and drive with the animals, and Sandy will fly down in Sarah and Eddie's Palatus on the 9th. [*Sarah Richardson and Eddie Franco are dear friends from the Mountain and are among the many who were so extraordinary throughout this ordeal. After Sandy died they flew several of us from Florida to New York and back for her funeral.*] Her trip will be two hours compared to two days—not bad. In any event, Please remove us from your e-mail list until around the 15th. No jokes, no chain e-mails or inspirational messages or "If I don't get this back I'll know you always secretly hated me" messages (the last three, EVER). No nothing except to tell me you just read my obituary and want to know if it's true. Thanks. We'll be online for this week, but it's going to be a difficult time, as you can well imagine. Thanks much.

New Year's Eve we went to a black-tie affair, but Sandy

had just finished chemo on the 12th of December and didn't feel well. On top of that the band was lousy. It was to be the last time we would go out on a New Year's Eve.

The First Recurrence

JANUARY 20, 2006

As some of you know, Sandy had a CT (Computed Tomography) scan, or CAT (Computed Axial Tomography), last week as a routine precaution. It showed a cancerous lesion at the T9 vertebra pushing on her spinal cord, which explains the back pain she's been having for the past month. Yesterday she had a PET (Positron Emission Tomography) scan which showed an additional small cancer in the lower left lobe of her lung, on the opposite side from the original lung cancer. This one is very small and brand new. The one in her spine has been there all along but was too small to be picked up on the bone scan last July. Nobody can explain why the chemo didn't get these two. The good news is that it is nowhere else in her body, and these two can be treated by aggressive radiation. There is a surgical option, but we consider it a last resort because they said they won't be able to get it all that way due to the proximity to the spinal cord and the risk of paralysis. She will have a needle biopsy next Thursday, and they will insert a metal marker in her spine so that they can pinpoint the radiation.

While the reappearance of the cancer is devastating, at least it's contained and should prove treatable. As you know, Sandy is strong and has a magnificent attitude. Once again, we think we got lucky with our bad luck. I'll keep you informed. Your good thoughts and prayers will get her though this one too.

JANUARY 30, 2006

We just got the results of the pathology and, as expected, it shows a malignancy in her spine at the T10 vertebra of the same type of cancer that was removed from her lung last summer. We will treat it by radiation starting no later than next week. We are, of course, disappointed that all that chemo did not get this and the other spot that was discovered in her lower left lung. We are told that the reason is that they are so slow growing and inactive that the chemo doesn't get them. That's kind of a good news/ bad news thing. The oncologist said that based on the same information he had two days ago, when he told us how good it was that it was only in two spots, on Friday he said that it had to travel to those spots via her bloodstream, so it's like grains of sand that could have dropped microscopic spots all along the way that haven't shown up yet. We will have her checked regularly, and if that happens, we'll deal with it. The first thing is to take care of the one on her spine because it's pressing on her spinal cord and could cause her the loss of the use of her legs. Sandy, as you all know, is tremendously strong and has an amazing attitude. Not only are we going to beat this and anything else life throws at us, but we have every intention of dying together at the age of 101, in bed, in a compromising position, giving all of you who are left and can dodder to our funeral REALLY something to talk about over the finger sandwiches, coffee, tea, and wine—lots and lots of wine.

On February 4th we threw a big party. Our new Naples

neighbors were there, along with friends from the Around the World trip who came from Sarasota. Our Mountain friends came from all over Florida and we even had people come from New York. It was a great time. Sandy, as always, was the perfect hostess.

FEBRUARY 8, 2006

Sandy was going to start radiation with a triangulation machine called Trilogy, and had already had an acrylic marker inserted in her back when she had a needle biopsy last week, when we got some interesting news. Friends of ours learned of a new device called a Cyberknife. We researched it, and it's totally state-of-the-art. It's also only in use in sixteen places in the country so far, but amazingly Naples is one of them. We decided we would use the Cyberknife as opposed to the Trilogy machine.

Yesterday, Sandy had two metal screws placed in her spine as markers, and today she had a CT scan to plan the radiation precisely. It should start Tuesday and consist of five days of intense treatments. If we're lucky, it'll destroy the tumor and relieve the pressure on her spinal cord. After that she'll have to do chemo again to get rid of the new tumor in her lung. We're very hopeful that this will do the trick. Her hair is just starting to grow in (dark), but the new chemo will mean starting over. We sure are getting an education that we never wanted.

FEBRUARY 10, 2006

This morning we went to an oncologist in Bonita Springs, Florida. Honestly, this guy could depress a hyena. Anyhow, he told us this was a very aggressive cancer, but the radiation should control and eliminate the tumor in her spine. A week later she will start chemo with a different cocktail. He was good enough to share that any of these chemos has only a fifteen to twenty percent chance of success. We're not crazy about those odds so we are also going to follow an aggressive holistic approach at the same time. Through our dear friends from New York, Dr. Bob and Susan Goldstein, we are being directed to the top holistic doctors in the country. The chemo will be for six months, max. We're doing this one step at a time and making sure that our Chardonnay budget keeps pace with our medical bills. The good news is that Sandy's overall excellent health works very strongly in her favor. Plus, she's absolutely petrified of the fact that if something happened to her I would be the one to pick out her clothes for the funeral. Trust me, that alone is enough of an incentive for her to live to be 101.

FEBRUARY 15, 2006

Sandy started radiation today with the Cyberknife. It's totally painless and amazingly precise. It took almost a week of planning, and the calculations have to be done by a physicist. The reason it has to be so exact is that the tumor is pressing on her spinal cord, which is causing a good deal of pain. If they were off by the slightest fraction, she could be left paralyzed from the waist down. Fortunately, everything went perfectly. Incredibly, there will only be three treatments, so by Friday afternoon we expect that tumor to be gone—though it may be a couple of weeks while the bone heals before she's pain free. After that we have to deal with a spot in her cervical spine that has created a difference of opinion. One radiologist thinks it's a tumor, others aren't sure. It's a collapsed vertebra, which may also be the result of an episode of whiplash last fall, or osteoporosis. We're getting old X-rays to try to determine when it started because they all agree it looks old. If it turns out to be another tumor, it, too, can be dealt with by the Cyberknife, although it's a bit more tricky. Once she's done with the radiation she will have to do chemo for about six months. We are also going to go the holistic route at the same time. Her attitude is phenomenal as you would expect because, after all, she's Sandy.

FEBRUARY 20, 2006

Friday was the third and final Cyberknife radiation treatment for the tumor in Sandy's spine, and although she's still in quite a bit of pain, hopefully the tumor is gone. That will be confirmed once the swelling goes down. Tomorrow she'll have a bone scan to see what more can be determined about the problem at C-3 in her neck. We know it's a fracture, but nobody is yet sure what it's attributable to. It has to be stabilized, which means an operation. It's very tricky because of where it is. We're told it's also quite painful, but there is no real choice—and it needs to be done very soon. It requires two to three nights in the hospital, and three to four weeks of recuperation—but after that she'll at least be able to play golf again. Another theory of how this thing was fractured is that it could be from her hitting herself in the neck with her backswing all those years. We should know more by the end of the week. If there is a tumor there, it can be treated by the Cyberknife also. Any other cancer will be dealt with by chemo and building up her immune system through holistic nutrition and supplements so that it doesn't come back once we get rid of it.

MARCH 2, 2006

Sandy's surgery yesterday went well. Our great friends from the Mountain, Howell and Beverly Hammond, came and stayed with me the entire day at the hospital. They've stabilized her neck with four screws, two rods, and cadaver paste (Ugh). They also put in two markers in case she needs Cyberknife radiation at that spot. They were unable to biopsy the collapsed vertebra because of the location, but they believe it was caused by a tumor that was not there in September and did not show up on the PET scan last month. If it is a tumor, they don't know if it's a live tumor or one that was killed by the chemo, and because of where it was it caused the vertebra to fracture and collapse and that's why it didn't show up on the PET scan. We'll cross that bridge later. She'll be in the hospital another day or two until she can manage the pain with just pills. Today will be bad, we were told. We both had a very bad feeling about this surgery, but it was just our fear manifesting itself.

To make yesterday the real emotional roller coaster that it was, it ended on a real high when our son Mark's wife, Hallie, presented us with our third grandchild, Jack Isaac Benson. Also, our lifelong friends Bobby and Phyllis Ciovacco became grandparents for the first time. Thank you all for your support, your good wishes, and your prayers from New York to Texas to Florida to California to Hanoi, of all places. Sandy and I are truly blessed to have all of you creating such positive energy for us. We can feel it even at the darkest of times. We'll see the holistic nutritionist next week, and when she heals we'll have to do chemo again. If there is still some cancer, we'll opt for proton radiation. Of course, first we've got to get Sandy home and ready to party again.

MARCH 3, 2006

Hooray, hooray, I brought her home today!!!!!! I think she fudged her answers to the docs a little bit (Okay, maybe more than a little bit), but she was able to get herself sprung from the joint. I think she may reconsider, though, when after the first meal I cook for her she starts to yearn for hospital food again. She's in a neck brace and the pain is quite bad, but hopefully it'll ease off in a day or so. The dog and the cat were so excited to see her that they stayed awake for almost fifteen minutes straight. One day at a time. I'm just thrilled to have her home.

MARCH 4, 2006

I have no intention of making this a daily missive, but Sandy is home and resting. She has twenty-two metal staples extending from the base of her skull down to the nape of her neck. She was allergic to the dressing so a doctor friend from the Mountain came over, removed the dressing, and applied antibiotic cream to the wound. I, the Hunter-Gatherer of our clan, went into the wilds of Naples to provide sustenance for our little tribe. We think Sandy is feeling a bit better because she's whining a bit more. As a matter of fact, under the heading of "lines I wish I had come up with" yesterday, before Sandy left the hospital she was talking to the neurosurgeon who performed the operation and was, shall we say, regaling him with her aches and pains. All of a sudden she stopped and said, "I'm whining, aren't I?" He replied, without batting an eye, "Would you like cheese with that?" Gotta love it. And with that, to all a good night.

APRIL 1, 2006

We finally heard from the doctor about the MRI last night. Of course, there is never a definitive answer to anything, but as far as we can gather, it's good news. The tumor in her spine is still there, which was expected, but has a hollow space in it from the Cyberknife. While it hasn't shrunk, it also hasn't grown, which is good. There is no sign of collapsed vertebrae, which is very good—although there is still a risk of that happening. The intense pain she's experiencing in her back and her neck is normal, so they gave her muscle relaxants because the pain is preventing healing. If she feels well enough, the next round of chemo will begin on the 17th. Nobody knows if there is cancer or not, but we have to proceed as if there is, hence the chemo. When she is able, we also will go to Boston to see an Eastern medicine expert and will continue pursuing a holistic approach. We were fortunate enough to have friends from both Houston and Santa Fe visit us over the last couple of weeks, along with several of our Mountain friends the other evening, all of which did Sandy a world of good, even through all the pain. For the next couple of weeks she just has to rest up to get strong enough for the chemo. Everybody keeps coming up with great food to make sure she eats properly. She's thin, but doing all right. I, of course, will soon need to get rolled down the street.

APRIL 14, 2006

The biggest problem these days is the pain Sandy is in. She has been waking up in tears and cries from it several times a day. We are told the pain is entirely normal, although we were originally told that in two to four weeks after surgery everything would be fine. The solution has been to drug her to the point of stupefaction. She either has to endure the pain (Sandy has a very high pain threshold, so it must be excruciating) or allow her to be on the verge of comatose. Today we went to a pain management doctor who has suggested some things to get her off of, or at least cut back on, the heavy-duty drugs. She has trouble functioning at all. This is a woman who speaks three languages (four if you include Texan), has advanced degrees, and has a genius-level IQ (just one point below mine, I must admit, although innate modesty precludes me from mentioning it). She has been having trouble putting two words together over the last couple of weeks. She's supposed to start chemo again on Monday, but it's highly unlikely. If this other stuff starts to work, however, she may be able to start it sometime next week.

The week after next, four of her childhood friends from Aransas Pass, Texas, are coming to visit. Gloria Peer, Darlene Boehnke, Linda Lee Dupnick, and Sandra LaBaume are people whom she loves dearly. I think this will be a great shot in the arm for her. I think that returning to the Mountain the second weekend in May will also provide a much needed boost. I know this has been wordy, and we

29

thank all of you for caring enough to listen. She knows she's surrounded by love and prayers from all over the country. We feel lucky and honored to know each of you.

APRIL 21, 2006

On Friday, during a routine CT scan to determinate how Sandy's neck was to be radiated, they found a swelling in her brain. An MRI today determined that there are two cancerous lesions in her brain in the area that controls motor function, which explains some balance problems she's been having lately. We're exploring our options, but will probably elect Cyberknife radiation since it's immediately available both here and in Asheville. Having her friends here from Texas for a couple of days is a great comfort, but I must admit I forgot how much these girls can drink. Dinner last night was a small fortune, and none of them ate anything but appetizers and salads. I made the mistake of having my blood pressure taken this morning. I finally found something higher than my weight. We'll keep you all informed as we attack this thing and beat it.

APRIL 25, 2006

We are going to start radiation tomorrow afternoon after the Texans leave and we start to sober up. The radiation oncologist told Sandy today that she intends to send her back to North Carolina with a clean bill of health. She's going to radiate the brain lesions and her neck area. It's a ten-day program but doesn't have to be every day. We don't know if she's blowing smoke, but since that conversation Sandy's entire attitude brightened for the better (mine too). We have one more night of alcoholic oblivion, and then we get serious about getting rid of this stuff. Sandy has had a great day since that phone call. We would like you all to have a drink to her health tonight, and we'll have one too. This goes to over one hundred people in thirty-five states, so we may have a VERY long evening if we're to toast with each of you—and we wouldn't insult any of you by leaving you out.

APRIL 28, 2006

Finally, something other than bad news. Yesterday, Sandy had chemo in the morning, followed by an MRI, followed by radiation. The MRI was because she was having so much pain in her thoracic spine where they did the Cyberknife surgery a couple of months ago. Because of the pain, they were pretty sure that the tumor was growing and the Cyberknife didn't work. We just found out that there is no tumor growth, meaning that the Cyberknife worked and the tumor is either dead or dying. The pain is from the three next lowest vertebrae, which are protruding. Not many people would get excited about protruding discs, but we're thrilled. We are also set up with an oncologist in North Carolina for the chemo and with a radiation oncologist in Asheville who will perform the Cyberknife surgery on the two brain lesions and will take her as soon as she gets back to the Mountain in a couple of weeks.

In the meantime, we are trying to keep her immune system working well through good (or not so bad) nutrition. So far her blood count remains excellent in spite of the chemo and the radiation. She eats pretty well and has maintained her weight at 108. Of course, let's face it, people have pets that weigh more. Throughout all this

I have also managed to maintain, and even substantially increase, my own weight. It helps, however, during the rare occasions that I've gotten to play golf. I use the scientific principle of centrifugal belly. In other words, a belly that starts in motion tends to stay in motion. It is the total principle governing my follow-through. Here's wishing all of you a good weekend. We fully expect to have a good one also.

MAY 15, 2006

We just returned from a full day of meetings in Asheville with the new oncologist and radiation oncologist. Tomorrow we meet with the neurosurgeon to plan the Cyberknife surgery for next Wednesday the 23rd. They feel there is a better than ninety percent chance of getting both the brain tumors. They both told us what we already know—metastatic lung cancer is incurable. The issue is controlling it, because it will continue to reoccur. When it settles in the bone it becomes very hard to measure, and that is what has partially happened. We will simply have to deal with it as it arises, and we intend to take an alternate approach this summer to go along with traditional treatment measures. We're happy to be back on the Mountain where we have so many friends and such an amazing support group. It hasn't exactly been fun, but we still try to find things to laugh about every day. This Wednesday is six hours of chemo, but then we go to the airport to pick up our grandchildren, Sophia and Jack. We've never met Jack. They're bringing their parents to see us. It's going to be a fabulous few days.

MAY 25, 2006

The Cyberknife surgery on Sandy's two brain tumors yesterday went well but, unlike traditional surgery, we will have to wait a couple of months to determine the success of the procedure. It doesn't immediately eliminate the tumors, it slices them up to prevent growth and then, hopefully, they begin to die and in a year or so disappear completely.

It took a while to get the results of last Tuesday's MRI to determine the cause of the pain in her back and left side. The obvious concern was spread of the tumor. The radiology tech read the MRI right away, but he, of course, will speak only to God. In spite of my numerous phone calls to On High on Tuesday afternoon and Wednesday morning, God was, according to his nurse, quite busy. Finally, however, God said, "Let there be a phone call," and Lo, there was indeed a phone call. I was able to speak directly to the Omnipotent One himself. Although absolute commitment are words that do not exist in any medical dictionary, we were told that there is no additional tumor in her back, and a comparison later today with a previous MRI will determine if the existing tumor has stabilized or shrunk. The pain is from the three herniated discs directly below T-10, which have protruded from the swelling associated with the earlier Cyberknife surgery and are pressing on her spinal cord and nerves. We expect to deal with this on a temporary basis with a long-term epidural until Sandy is strong enough to withstand surgery. Additional good news is that her blood work is excellent and she does not need any boosters to help her withstand the chemo at this time.

There probably are not many people who would celebrate having three herniated discs, but we went to dinner at the Savoy, an excellent restaurant in Asheville, after the Cyberknife, and Sandy had two cosmos and a big dinner. Little by little we're coming back from this thing. I know I may have offended some of you with what I wrote here, but I figure that God gave us a sense of humor in order to do more with it than just forward e-mail jokes. Sandy and I find things to laugh at every day, sometimes through tears. It really is the best medicine, along with our being so lucky as to have so many friends and family from all over the country who surround us with so much love.

MAY 28, 2006

It seems as though every time we get up, we get whacked again. It seems that the tumor in Sandy's spine that was treated by Cyberknife in February has swelled, which was not unexpected, and although it is probably dying, it has wrapped itself around her spinal cord and is compressing it. The danger is that if it shrinks—as hoped—it will compress more and can cause permanent paralysis. They want to do surgery on Wednesday to try to remove it. Obviously this is major surgery, and since it involves the spinal cord, it is quite dangerous. It also means interrupting the chemo regimen, so she will probably have to repeat it in a few weeks. We've contacted her doctors in Florida, and the neurosurgeon here in Asheville will consult with them this morning. We will do this if they all come out on the same page, and although the guy here has a great reputation, we're not about to take his solo prognosis of Tuesday's MRI as gospel. He is saying that the pain in her back and left side is a result of the tumor, not the herniated discs. This is all crushing, but we'll get through it. We'll get through anything that this throws at us.

On the upside, we danced last night for the first time since November and got to see a whole bunch of our Mountain friends. All this stuff is really interfering with our party time.

Sandy had the spinal surgery yesterday. The surgeon removed two vertebrae (T-10 & T-11), and replaced them with cadaver bone from the bone bank, then stabilized them with rods and screws. We were told this would be extremely painful, and Sandy has periodically been in excruciating pain, even through the morphine. I stayed in the chair next to her bed last night and only just came home to get a few things, send this, and shower and change clothes. I decided I might be a bit too funky when the hospital cleaning crew sprayed me with Lysol and asked me to move to the quarantine area. I'm heading back to Asheville shortly and will spend the night with her again. The nurses are amazed at her spirit. They said she must be a real live wire when she's feeling well. They don't know the half of it.

JUNE 5, 2006

I brought Sandy home from the hospital late this afternoon after six days. I stayed with her there every night, sleeping in the green genuine-plastic chair by her bed. Ordinarily, if you saw a person sleeping in their clothes in a green genuine-plastic chair every night you would consider that person a homeless vagrant. At best. I was able to come home for a couple of hours every other day to shower and change clothes only through the kindness of our dear friends Beverly and Howell Hammond. One or both was at the hospital every day save one, and they kept B.B., our wandering Whippet, for us. Cleocatra had no problem staying home alone. Beverly and Howell are always there when needed. They came and sat with me the day of the surgery, as they did the day of Sandy's neck surgery in Florida in March. Amazing people.

I have learned how to live forever: Simply check into a hospital—any hospital will do. Once there, they won't let you close your eyes long enough to die. If they aren't checking Sandy's vital signs fourteen times a night, they are drawing out the few ounces of remaining blood. In addition, Sandy was hooked up to three wonderful, modern machines that beeped VERY loudly to continually remind us how hard they were working and how brilliant they were. One measured her respiration and beeped VERY loudly when her breaths per minute rose above or fell below a continuously changing preset number. Another one beeped VERY loudly when the morphine in the on-demand syringe was low, and the third beeped VERY loudly when, I am convinced, it sensed that nobody was jabbing, squeezing, or measuring her, or that the other two machines were resting their beepers. All in all, this was a very difficult ordeal.

JUNE 19, 2006

We just returned from Asheville, where Sandy had the staples removed and is thrilled. They took an X-ray of the spine area of the surgery, and the rods and screws all look fine and the wound will now start to heal. While a flat X-ray is not the ideal way of detecting cancer, we are cautiously optimistic because this showed no evidence of tumor. We know we may be grasping at straws, but it's great to at least have a straw to grasp. There will be an MRI on July 11th and a full bone scan on August 24th. Those will tell the tale. In the meantime, as some of you who were there know, we went to karaoke Saturday night and Sandy even danced (a bit) to "Mustang Sally." John and Linda Silvati returned to Cincinnati yesterday after a fabulous ten-day visit. We may have knocked them out. The people on the Mountain continue to astound us with their kindness and generosity. This would have been much tougher to deal with someplace else.

JULY 3, 2006

As we are about to celebrate the 230th birthday of the United States, I thought I might share an incident with you that occurred at the Bicentennial celebration in New York, thirty years ago tomorrow. I had friends who lived on the West Side of Manhattan, and I had gone to the city to watch the parade of the Tall Ships up the Hudson, which I did from the shoreline at 72nd Street. That evening, we all went downtown to watch the fireworks over the Statue of Liberty. I became separated from the Group and settled down on the sand in the area that later was developed as Battery Park City along with tens if not hundreds of thousands of people. The fireworks were, to say the least, breathtakingly spectacular. The climax was a giant American flag shot off over the Statue of Liberty. At that point, a young man about twenty yards to my left stood up. He was thin with black, curly hair, wearing jeans, a T-shirt, and a backpack. In an absolutely magnificent, clear voice, he started to sing "The Star Spangled Banner." Little by little, people stood up and started singing with him until there were thousands of us singing as the flag blazed above the Statue. There were people from all over the world who raised their voices together in a spontaneous celebration of 200 years of freedom and opportunity. It gave me chills then. It still gives me chills even now. Happy Birthday to us all.

JULY 14, 2006

Sorry we've been out of touch for a week or so. Our computer was at a rest home in California suffering from, as I understand it, Computile Paralastic Dementia aggravated by Degenerative Cyberphoric Calasamatation. It returned home this afternoon to a rousing welcome, and 108 emails.

Sandy had an MRI this past Tuesday on her thoracic and lumbar spine areas. Her lumbar spine is clear. The tumor remains in her thoracic spine but it has not grown at all. This would indicate that the oral chemo she started five weeks ago, Tarceva, is working. This is the first time in seven months that there has been no spread and no growth. Needless to say, we're absolutely giddy.

There will be a full bone, brain, and CT scan on August 24th. Each day brings us closer to something that will work indefinitely. We're going to Boston on the 31st to meet with a holistic doctor so we can try to combine the best of both Eastern and Western medicines. We are, at this point, cautiously optimistic. Sandy's spirits are great, and she looks, as always, fantastic. I truly live by reflected glory.

July 30, 2006

We leave tomorrow for Boston to see a holistic doctor to see if we can combine Eastern medicine with what we've been doing to this point and hopefully build up Sandy's immune system enough so that it can fight this thing and get rid of it. Our friends Sarah Richardson and Eddie Franco are flying us to and from the Mountain and, while in Boston, we'll be staying on their boat. We're being met in Boston by our longtime friends from New York, Dr. Bob and Susan Goldstein, internationally known due to their holistic work with animals—particularly cancer. They have offered to go to the consultation with us. This way there will be people there who understand what's being said and can advise us as to the usefulness of what's being proposed.

After the last MRI showed that the tumor in her spine had not grown, Sandy had a chest X-ray and it showed that her lungs are clear. Our main concern of late has been her weight. She was down to ninety-five pounds but has started water exercises and has been eating like a horse and has put on about six pounds. If I ate the way she's been eating, I'd be as big as a house. Actually, I AM as big as a house.

August 2, 2006

We just returned from Boston. Sandy clicked with the holistic doctor immediately. As briefly as possible, he tested her and had blood drawn. The good news is that her organs are in excellent condition, especially her liver. Needless to say, we were all shocked. The bad news is that the portion of her immune system that she needs to manufacture the cells to fight the cancer has been destroyed by the chemo and the radiation, and she can't manufacture them on her own. Within a couple of weeks, however, he will have put together a program that will have her manufacturing these cells on her own. Fortunately, Dr. Bob and Susan Goldstein were with us, because I don't think I could have otherwise followed it all. The next big hurdle is all the scans toward the end of August, and then it's back to Boston for a week or two so Sandy can get intensive treatment from this doctor. Hopefully the combination of Eastern and Western medicines will have a totally positive effect.

AUGUST 19, 2006

We saw the oncologist yesterday and got the result of Tuesday's bone, brain, and CT scans. According to the doctor, the tumor, if it's still there, has not grown, may have shrunk, or may not be there at all. There is no evidence of tumor anywhere else in her body. Yesterday was our anniversary and, needless to say, we could not have gotten a better present. Sandy will be checked by scans again in late October, but until then we can breathe again and live normally. Although we know that the oral chemo she's taking doesn't work forever, perhaps a year to eighteen months, each day is a gift and a chance to find something that will work permanently. Providing I can find a way to get her there, Sandy will leave Tuesday for three weeks in a holistic clinic in Boston to build up her immune system so that she can once again manufacture the cells that fight cancer.

Maybe now my blood pressure, which until this started fourteen months ago was always 120 over 80 but now is higher than my weight, can get down a bit. The other day, when I checked it on a blood pressure machine in a supermarket while waiting for them to fill one of Sandy's prescriptions, the results screen had one of those crawly things go across it, like they have on CNN. It said, "Please remove your arm from the sleeve, go out and get in your car, drive directly to the morgue, go inside, open up one of those little doors, lie down on the 'rolling thingee', roll yourself in, and pull the little door closed after you." Okay, I can take a hint. In any event, thank all of you for your wonderful support, healing thoughts, prayers, and good wishes. The odds against any kind of a victory were astronomical. Thank you for fighting this fight with us. Yesterday we were all winners.

SEPTEMBER 7, 2006

Sandy will come home late Saturday from the holistic clinic in Boston. We really are not sure if this has helped or if it weakened her even further. She got to see dear old friends, Eddie and Norine Corbo from Connecticut and Ron and Sulli Seger from Maine, so that was a positive thing. The dog, the cat, and I can't wait. Our friend from the Mountain, Doug Pilkington, is flying her back to the Mountain. She's doing well and is determined to follow through with the regimen she's been put on, which is a combination of a macrobiotic diet, herbs, and a specially formulated tea. We got the results of the latest blood work back yesterday, though, and they are discouraging. Her lymphocytes and T cells, the cancer-fighting agents, are down by nine percent, and the cancer cells (CEA) are up by almost sixty percent. We know this program can take three months to kick in, but we were hoping for better results. Sandy feels fine in every other way, although she still has pain in her neck and back. This is just one more obstacle to get over.

SEPTEMBER 14, 2006

Yesterday, September 13th, would have been my father's ninety-seventh birthday were he alive, but he's not so it wasn't. It wasn't a very good day for us, unfortunately. Sandy had a thoracic and a cervical MRI. They showed that the tumor in her spine is growing out along her rib and that there is a new tumor at the T-3 vertebra. The doctors also think there are peripheral spots in her lungs and liver. They have thought this before, and subsequent tests have shown those areas to be clear, so we'll wait for more definitive tests before we worry too much.

The cancer she has is an undifferentiated carcinoma, and is very aggressive. The good news is that the new tumor at T-3 can still be treated with Cyberknife radiation. It has not yet closed around the spinal cord the way the one at T-10 had. The surgery will be done next week or the week after with a high degree of confidence that it will be as successful as the Cyberknife surgery to get rid of the two brain tumors was last May. Sandy commented yesterday that she's in big trouble. Of course she is, and we both know it, but I keep telling her that although something's going to get us all it's not going to be this, and it's not going to be now.

SEPTEMBER 29, 2006

Sandy had her third Cyberknife surgery on Wednesday to go along with the three major invasive surgeries over the past fourteen months. This one was to get the new tumor that appeared at T-3. We won't know if it worked until she has an MRI when we return to Florida in early November. She's been in terrible pain, but hopefully she will start to get some relief in her upper spine now. She stopped taking chemo three days ago since it wasn't working, and we need to give the holistic regimen a chance to build up her immune system over the next couple of months. While it's supposed to build up her immune system, it's causing her to lose weight. She's down to one hundred pounds, and as a result is getting weaker. Somewhere out there is a happy medium. We'll keep searching. We're extremely lucky to be surrounded by the most fantastic people here on the Mountain and our myriad friends around the country. We keep on boogying, but the music is just a bit slower for now.

OCTOBER 1, 2006

After two nights of not sleeping and Sandy being in absolute agony, we finally went to the emergency room in Asheville yesterday for a fun-filled day. Sandy has got to be the only person who, in spite of being in tears from pain, insisted on bathing and putting on makeup for a trip to the emergency room.

There was good news and bad news. The bad news is that after spending the day there they have no idea what's causing the pain. It may be muscular, because the good news is that it's not the cancer. They gave her an MRI and a chest X-ray and found everything the same as before, no new tumors and what she's got has not progressed. It's too early to tell the effects of Wednesday's Cyberknife. I think the pain may be associated with the triple dose of radiation from the Cyberknife which almost certainly had to cause some temporary nerve damage. The chest X-Ray showed nodules on her lungs, but they have not changed since last time. She is modifying the macrobiotic diet because it was weakening her too badly. She'll stick with the herbs and herbal tea, and will continue to avoid processed sugar where possible, but will start to eat bread and dairy products. She's still in a lot of pain this morning and is taking hydrocodon. At the hospital they gave her morphine and hydrocodon, so she was a bit more loopy than usual when we got home last night. There was a party we very much wanted to go to. It was all our favorite things—singing, dancing, food, booze, and good friends—but even for us, this would have been over the top. We actually momentarily considered it though, on our way up the Mountain last night. Someday we'll probably have to grow up, but not just yet.

October 10, 2006

Sandy had a CT scan and a PET scan yesterday. We then went to see Doctor Doom, the oncologist. This guy could depress a hyena. He didn't know that she had been to the ER or that she had gotten an MRI or that she had the scans yesterday before seeing him. He pulled it up on a computer, and although it hadn't been read by a radiologist, he gave us the benefit of his opinion. He thinks it's spread to her liver and her kidneys. We won't know for sure until later today. To make us feel even more warm and fuzzy, he told us that it was incurable from the moment it metastasized out of her lung, which was before it was even diagnosed. He told us the best we can hope for is to slow it down and maybe even halt its progress, but it's very aggressive. He said it almost certainly will not go into remission. He might as well have just shot us. In spite of him, we're not ready to roll over.

Sandy is taking pain pills and acupuncture and it's helping slightly. She will start a different form of chemo tomorrow. Each different chemo has no more than a twenty to twenty-five percent chance of being effective. This will be the fourth one we've tried. There are new things coming out all the time and we will continue to follow every possibility that seems semi-sane. She will continue to avoid sugars and processed foods, but overall the macrobiotic diet has been disappointing. She's down to ninety-six pounds in spite of the fact that her appetite is good and she's eating. I'm trying to do my part by eating as much as I can, but she hasn't started to gain weight yet. She will start to eat several small meals a day and will include potatoes and some other starches. Hopefully we'll start to see some improvement. She's lost twenty pounds since May and eleven of them are since she started this diet. We've got to get her back to the point where her skin fits again.

OCTOBER 13, 2006

Yesterday I finally called the radiation oncologist since Doctor Doom never called us back about the scans. I suspect it was because, although the news was bad, it was not quite as bad as he told us before the scans were read by a radiologist and therefore he might have had to soften his morbid pronouncements slightly. The cancer has indeed now spread to Sandy's liver, and the tumor is sizable. It has not, however, spread to her kidneys as we were originally told. We do, however, in spite of this news, see the first slight glimmer of hope. Friends of ours here on the Mountain, Ralph and Debbie Muller, have friends in Mississippi who have just had a miraculous recovery from stage 4 brain cancer. The treatment was the introduction of stem cells (the procedure was not done in the U.S.). If that offends anyone's beliefs, it can't be helped and I make no apology for it. He went from stage 4 to being cancer free. We are checking this procedure and the administration of it through a few outside sources and are getting all the details. It's an hour-long, painless procedure that is administered either intravenously or subcutaneously. If anyone has trouble with the meaning of that word I would refer you to a dictionary, as long as it is NOT one that includes words like "y'all," "mightcoulda," and "used-tawuz." We will update you when we know more. In the meantime, Sandy is still in great pain (the doctors cannot explain the pain at the site of the last Cyberknife surgery, or the pain in her right shoulder) and will continue with traditional systemic treatment. We thank all of you for your heartwarming interest and incredible support.

OCTOBER 17, 2006

We have made all the arrangements to go to the Dominican Republic so that Sandy can have stem cell therapy on October 27th. What it will do is boost her immune system by about one thousand percent. This was the object of the three weeks at the holistic clinic in Boston, but this is much faster and much more intense. We don't think we have the time to let her immune system build slowly with herbs, teas, etc. In addition, after we return we will meet with a radiologist in Greenwood, Mississippi, who is doing very innovative things. He was recommended by the doctor who does the stem cell therapy at a small private hospital in the Dominican Republic. We had an extensive phone conversation with him last night. We are certainly cautiously optimistic. I just learned a statistic that I'm glad I didn't know sixteen months ago when Sandy was first diagnosed. It seems that fifty-eight percent of all people diagnosed with lung cancer die within the first year. Sandy has now outlived approximately sixty-five percent of people diagnosed with lung cancer. Of course, the fact that it has reached her liver is not to be discounted. She is still experiencing a tremendous amount of pain and nausea. We have canceled any more chemo. It is so destructive to the immune system that it can be fatal no matter what it does to the tumors. It's barbaric. I was mistaken last week when I said she weighed ninety-six pounds. It's ninety-two pounds, and she's so nauseous she can't eat much some days, although her appetite is good. She thinks she looks horrible at ninety-two pounds. When I first met her on August 18, 1982, she weighed eighty-nine pounds and she thought she looked great. So help me, I'll never understand women.

The 27th should be a lucky day for us. We were married in Texas on August 18, 1985, but then we had a second wedding in New York at our home in Pound Ridge for the rest of the rabble on October 27th. It had been cold and we planned to have it indoors but that day dawned bright and beautiful and we had a lovely ceremony outdoors overlooking the lake. It was a small miracle because the next day there was a hard freeze. It's time for another small miracle, although, as our dear friend from New York, Norine Corbo said, "We don't need a miracle. Sandy is a little miracle all by herself."

OCTOBER 18, 2006

Many of you either remember Sandy's famous "kick ass" line on the way to Ireland in September 2004 or have heard about it. In the long conversation with the stem cell doctor the other night, he made what was a really odd remark to people he'd never met (us). These are direct quotes. He said, at one point, "Many times I can tell who's going to live and who's going to die just from speaking with them. You're going to live." Toward the end of the conversation he said to Sandy, "You are going to kick ass." If there's any kind of a sign, that's got to be it.

OCTOBER 30, 2006

We got back from the Dominican Republic last night and, if this works, Sandy has a new immune system. The next thing to do is to get her to the radiologist in Mississippi who has a drug that will rejuvenate her own immune system and, between them, she can hopefully defeat this thing. The people in the Dominican Republic have been doing this for eleven years and the radiologist has been doing this for five years. Every one of his patients remains alive, including those who were only given a matter of months to live.

This afternoon we will have an X-ray done of her right shoulder and neck where she has been experiencing worsening pain since she was in Boston. The doctors here shrug it off to the cancer, but there is no cancer in those areas, so it's time to find out what the problem is and correct it. The actual procedure took an hour and a half and involved one shot in her arm and four in her side. Those were painful. The rest of the time we were in the Dominican Republic (a total of forty-nine hours) we stayed at Casa de Campo exploring the resort and trying to relax as much as possible. We flew into Miami Saturday evening, and Doug and Shelby Pilkington from the Mountain picked us up and took us to the Riviera Country Club for dinner. It was lovely and very gracious of them. As usual, we managed to make the best of a difficult and stressful situation and had some laughs in the process. Now we just have to hope this all works. Of course, now I have to get Sandy to Greenwood, Mississippi, which is somewhat off our normal beaten path.

NOVEMBER 3, 2006

Yesterday, I flew with Sandy to Greenwood, Mississippi to spend three weeks there. I flew back to the Mountain to get the house closed up, the vehicles shipped to Florida, etc., and will join her on Tuesday. The purpose of this is to rejuvenate her immune system to add to the new immune system she got in the Dominican Republic last week. In addition, they use an Austrian drug called Ukrain which greatly enhances the body's ability to create T cells, which directly attack cancer cells. The drug is not yet FDA approved, but it is approved for use as the FDA studies it. This is all basically immunotherapy. The credentials of the doctor in charge of the North Central Mississippi Regional Cancer Center are excellent. We have very high hopes that this, combined with the stem cell therapy, will put this thing into remission, against huge odds.

It is very frustrating to know that most doctors know about these treatments but never say a word so they can proceed with their own agendas. Had we known about this a year and a half ago, Sandy would not have had to go through all the surgeries and pain, and it's quite possible that her life would now not be in such danger. Why is the center in Greenwood, Mississippi, you ask? No clue. You can learn more about it on their Web site, www.cancernet.com. By the way, I don't know if I can get a dial-up connection there, so PLEASE, starting Monday, no more e-mails until the 27th at the earliest. The only exception is that if you get absolute positive confirmation of my death, please let me know immediately. This is information I need.

NOVEMBER 5, 2006

Things change quickly. I was able to get out to Mississippi yesterday to join Sandy. Right now I've got a computer connection through Wi-Fi. Unfortunately we're staying in a dump, but it's the only place in Greenwood that takes animals and we have both B.B. and Cleocatra with us. Howell and Beverly Hammond from the Mountain not only facilitated my being able to fly out here three days ahead of schedule, but also flew out here with me yesterday and flew back to North Carolina last night in order to see Sandy for five minutes at the airport. Truly amazing friends.

Sandy met with the doctor on Friday and he has outlined a course of treatment for her. Tomorrow (Monday) she will have a CT scan and lab work. Obviously we have high hopes for this, combined with what we did last week in the Dominican Republic. Sandy has gained some weight—up to ninety-six from a low of ninety pounds— so that's a good thing. The bad thing is that I'm eating all the same stuff she is. Draw your own conclusions.

NOVEMBER 10, 2006

Sandy has had a couple of treatments of the drug Ukrain, and we will have an indication next week when they do another CEA (cancer cell count) as to how it's working. Her CEA the day before the first treatment was 1,314.37. Before she went to the clinic in Boston in August it was in the 400s, and after the first two weeks there it was in the 700s. To put that in perspective, ninety-seven percent of healthy non-smokers have a CEA of 3.0 or less and only five percent of healthy smokers (now there's an oxymoron) have a CEA of as much as 1 to 10. If her CEA starts to move down it means the drug, in conjunction with the stem cell therapy, is working. The CT scan yesterday showed a large tumor in her liver. It's all in one place as opposed to spread throughout the liver, which is a good thing. The doctor suggested that it could be surgically removed, but after careful consideration and talking it over with folks, we've decided not to do it since we feel that any gain we would get from this treatment would be offset by the effort her body would have to put forth to recover.

Sandy will have a bone scan on Tuesday to try to determine the cause, once again, of the horrific pain in her neck. (Besides me, of course.) Other than her neck this is the third good day in a row that she's had. I don't remember the last time she had even two good days in a row. They've boosted her vitamin intake and she gives herself a daily shot of growth hormone. I don't really understand that. I've always thought she was quite tall enough. In the meantime, we remain here in our hovel in Greenwood, Mississippi. It meets my own personal 3-D standard: Depressing, Dirty, and Dilapidated. The dirty part bothers me most. As the old proverb comes close to saying, "Cleanliness is next to Artyness." The outside merely looks run down, but the front grass is at least cut. The back, however, is another story. To paraphrase Jeff Foxworthy, "if they ever cut the grass they might just find a car." However, the only way to get out of here is to shoot the dog and the cat, and Sandy would never let me get away with that. We continue to have great hopes that we can stop and reverse this cancer. Except for occasional meltdowns, Sandy's spirits are great. As our dear friend Boo Mortenson from Madison, Wisconsin, said after shopping with Sandy one day last winter in Naples, Florida, where she and Mort live ten minutes from us, "Sandy can't be THAT sick. She shops like she's going to live forever."

NOVEMBER 11, 2006

On Monday morning, Sandy will have a liver biopsy done. It will probably be laparoscopic, but requires general anesthesia. The reasoning is so stunningly simple that it's criminal that it's not done as a matter of course. What's amazing to me is that, as a matter of fact, it's not done at all, at least not in our experience. What happens is they will send a piece of liver to a lab, where it will be put into a petri dish. As the cancer cells grow, they will try different forms of medications, chemos, etc., to find what is effective against this particular cancer. Through these trials, they can determine what specific treatment this cancer needs. "Standard procedure," we've found, is for the oncologist to prescribe the "chemo du jour" and inject everyone with it for the course of the treatment, normally a few months, and if that doesn't work, start a new chemo regimen for a few months. Each chemo has no more than a twenty percent chance of being effective, and the percentage reduces with each new chemo used. In my opinion, this is akin to using patients' bodies as laboratories, resulting in running people out of time and out of life when it's possible to find something effective before the fact. If nothing else, Sandy will get better just to walk into Dr. Doom's office next summer and watch the little twerp's face when he thinks he's seeing a ghost.

The airport here in Greenwood, which has no commercial flights and where the sign was used for target practice by an obviously less-than-competent hunter, is an airplane graveyard. It's where DC 10s come to die. There are planes here from all over the world being scavenged for parts. Spain, Afghanistan, Arab countries, and one Useless Air 727 with blocks holding up the wings. Last night we went to one of the restaurants in town. You could tell it was fancy— some of the men had on sport coats over their GOOD jeans. Hot damn, it reminded me of New Year's Eve in Texas.

NOVEMBER 18, 2006

Sandy had the biopsy on Monday. We were told to be at the hospital at 6:45 A.M. which we were, and at 9:20 A.M., we were still sitting in the lobby as they tried to find her a bed. They are more than just a bit disorganized. I finally did a kind of New York thing and they suddenly found her a room. It didn't help much, since they didn't do the procedure until after 2:00 P.M. and we didn't leave the hospital until almost 6:00 P.M. It required three incisions—one at her navel, and two below her right rib cage. The samples were sent to a lab where they will, hopefully, find the proper treatment. Although her abdomen is sore, incredibly this is the second day in a row that she has no neck pain. We don't know why and are afraid to ask. The bone scan yesterday showed nothing new, so the only possibility is that all the new vitamins, minerals, and medications she has gotten here are starting to have an effect. We also think that there is a strong possibility that there is an oncologist in Naples who will follow this protocol using the Ukrain and the results of the lab work on the liver biopsy, along with the CEA markers denoting the level of cancer cells in her body. We learned of another woman from Naples who was treated here who has an oncologist who is doing that for her. This would be a tremendous blessing, since we desperately want to avoid returning here for a long period of time. It would mean not taking the animals with us because neither one of us can stand living in this place anymore. They've fumigated, but the roaches are winning. It's not just here. Last night they were running down the walls of the restaurant. The manager's comment was, "We do our best." Tonight, though, we're getting together with Charles and Jeannine White from the Mountain, who live in Clarksdale, Mississippi, about sixty miles north northwest of here, I think. Charles told me if I hadn't had called him he would have killed me. I told him that a lot of people think I need killing. It's very thoughtful of them to come all the way down here to see us, and we are truly looking forward to a normal social evening for the first time in the couple of weeks since we've been here. Mostly I just check the clock to see if it's late enough to have a drink yet. Lately 10:00 A.M. is starting to feel late enough.

NOVEMBER 19, 2006

We hope to have the results of the biopsy testing Monday or Tuesday. In the meantime, Sandy has started a 10-dose radiation procedure which will end at 8:30 A.M. Wednesday morning, just before we leave. That will be followed by the fourth administration of Ukrain. On the "very good news" side, there is a doctor in Bonita Springs, Florida, who will administer the Ukrain and follow the protocol prescribed by the doctor here in Mississippi. Sandy is also getting two types of oral chemo and has started on thalidomide. Many of us remember the horror of the thalidomide babies of the 1950s. It is being used as a cancer drug for the very reason it was so deadly all those years ago—it effectively chokes off the blood supply to the tumor, thereby helping to starve it. This may be a bit too graphic, but both a baby and a tumor are parasites that live off the host. The tumor in Sandy's liver is large and dangerous because the liver is like the Mother Lode, moving cells (cancerous or not) throughout the body via the bloodstream. In this case, as my father and his father before him used to say, "We've been lucky with our bad luck." There is very little arterial activity in this tumor, and whatever is there has a good chance to dissipate as the tumor shrinks from the radiation.

Unfortunately, the radiation has made Sandy quite sick and weak. She also continues to have horrific neck pain. Nothing shows up on any test, so nobody knows the reason. Personally, I think it must be nerve related since there doesn't seem to be any other explanation.

Dinner with Charles and Jeannine White from the Mountain was wonderful, and a very welcome respite. They even bought dinner. Talk about southern hospitality. It was particularly welcome now that we're on a fixed income. Our social security hardly even covers our bar bill. On a lighter note, we sold a condo in Texas this week and I called USAA to cancel the insurance. When I gave them my member number they informed me that I was dead. Naturally, I immediately asked to speak to a supervisor because news like that requires verification. It took a while, but apparently I'm not dead, much to my relief. That would have screwed up what is already a pretty lousy weekend. On Wednesday, Doug and Shelby Pilkington from the Mountain are going to pick us up in a Cessna 421 and take us with them to St. Simons Island, Georgia, to spend a couple of days with several Mountain couples at the home of Johnny and Peggy Capes. It will grieve us to leave here, of course. We'll miss the trains going through every hour of every day. We'll miss showering and shaving in cold water since there's barely enough hot water for one person. We'll miss the smell of the sewer treatment facility two doors down, and we'll certainly miss the not one, but two (!) plungers in the bathroom and the reason they're there. All this to say nothing of the dirt and the roaches and other insects that Cleocatra keeps trying to climb the walls to get at. Speaking of Cleocatra, she and the dog finally cooperated on something. After living in luxury for all these years they figured I finally hit bottom, as they always expected, so they put out a notice on the Internet that said, "New Owners Wanted. Pictures of accommodations must accompany all applications." Anyhow, just a few more days. As icing on the cake we just learned that John and Linda Silvati will come visit us in Naples the Tuesday after we get there. Seeing so many of our friends after this ordeal will be a great emotional boost. To those of you who send us e-mails, please hold off starting Tuesday for a week or so. It's going to be a bit hectic for a while. For those of you who've noticed that these e-mails have gotten progressively longer, you're right. It's because we're bored to tears.

NOVEMBER 21, 2006

This will be our last communication with you for a while. We are getting out of here tomorrow (Hallelujah). We may go out to the airport at midnight and wait. We do not yet have the results of the liver biopsy, but today they did a CEA (the blood test to measure the extent of the cancer). Fifteen days ago Sandy's was 1,314.37. Today it was 902.41, an incredible drop of approximately thirty-one percent in two weeks. The only difference is the Ukrain, plus some radiation, all on top of the stem cell therapy four weeks ago in the Dominican Republic. We've got a long, long way to go, but for the first time since this nightmare started seventeen months ago it's going in the right direction. Heat and radiation have alleviated some of Sandy's neck pain, too. We are going to CELEBRATE this Thanksgiving, and every other occasion we can come up with. We've tried to put as positive a spin on these e-mails as possible, but now, for the first time, we've actually got something positive to say. Thank you all for your incredible ongoing support.

NOVEMBER 28, 2006

We finally got to Florida, albeit by a rather circuitous route that led from North Carolina, through Mississippi, and then Georgia. Doug and Shelby Pilkington flew to Greenwood, picked us up, and flew us to St. Simons Island, Georgia, to the home of our old Mountain friends, Peggy and Johnny Capes, for a wonderful Thanksgiving, which turned out to be Sandy's last (strangely enough I'm writing this on Thanksgiving Day, 2011). Doug and Shelby then flew us to Florida. We got the results of the biopsy back about an hour before we left Mississippi (the reason I always spell out Mississippi is just to prove that I can spell Mississippi). They tested fifteen different chemos on the piece of the tumor that was removed. The categories of the tumor's resistance to each one were listed as Extreme, Intermediate, and Low. Of the fifteen chemotherapies, ten were extremely resistant, two were intermediate, and three offered only low resistance, one of which was the Ukrain, which would help to explain the more than thirty-one percent drop in the cancer cell count in just fifteen days. Of the ten extremely resistant chemos were all six that Sandy has been treated with previously. In other words, if they had done this same test a year and a half ago, or even at any point over the last year and a half, she would never have had to go through all the chemos and radiations and all the sickness and pain. They would have found out what worked and what didn't and only given her what worked against this particular cancer. If they had done the CEA testing to see if what they were doing was working or not, they would have been able to adjust what they were doing. This past summer Sandy asked Dr. Doom to do a CEA test when they drew blood for regular blood cell counts. He refused with no explanation. It's only by chance that we found that there are methodologies that may have a chance of saving Sandy's life. If we had been told about these things by our esteemed physicians at the outset, or anywhere along the way, there might not have been a reason for these e-mails. We hope you all had a great Thanksgiving. I'm told I had a fabulous one. Doug and Shelby Pilkington are our oldest friends on the Mountain Doug retired as a senior Captain for United Airlines and was in the air when 9/11 happened. Shelby retired after 25 years with Delta. Doug attended Coral Gables High School when Sandy was student-teaching French and Spanish there while attending the University of Miami. One evening on the Mountain, they traced it back and discovered that, when she was student-teaching at Coral Gables High School, Doug was in her Spanish class. I joked, "Gee Sandy, don't you remember a tall, bald, teen-ager with a gray mustache and goatee?" It's no surprise he didn't recognize her. Her name was different, her hair was different, and Sandy was one of those rare woman who got prettier and prettier as she got older.

DECEMBER 13, 2006

Physically, Sandy is amazingly better than last week. She had been in so much pain that she was ready to give up and

I was afraid to leave her alone. Now that we have a diagnosis, we know the neck pain is being caused by occipital neuralgia, which is not common and is very painful. (It was finally diagnosed.) The shots have relieved her tremendously, and are only making her slightly loopy and who could tell the difference. She got a shot of Ukrain and will get another one on Monday. The oncologist here has found a reputable doctor to administer the Ukrain. He can't do it (the oncologist) due to his corporate policy since it's not approved yet by the FDA. She had two infusions last week and one yesterday. The next is set for this Friday. At the same time, we will have blood redrawn for another CEA because the results of last Friday's just came back and they are awful. If there was no mistake, it cited her cancer cell count at 3,010, up over three times in the last three weeks. Even the oncologist's office thinks we need to test it again. It seems almost impossible. Sandy isn't home at the moment so it's going to be a bit touchy when she gets here. She's lost weight again—down to ninety two pounds—but is eating well and has a great appetite and a newfound love for Blue Bell brand Pecan, Pralines, and Cream ice cream with chocolate syrup. It seems to be working well on me too. We want to wish everyone Happy Holidays and a Happy and HEALTHY New Year.

DECEMBER 30, 2006

The year is ending on a bit of a downer. Sandy's CEA (cancer cell count) went up a little bit, and her red and white blood cell count, as well as her hemoglobin and platelet counts, went down. Her platelet count is well in the mid-range of acceptable, while the others are a bit low.

Her neck is bad, but we hope to get her a couple of shots next week to alleviate the pain. In the meantime, they have told her to double the pain meds, which are making her a bit loopy. Well, a bit loopier. She's kind of frail, weighing only ninety-three pounds fully dressed. Part of the problem is one of the oral chemos, Tarceva, that she's taking to sensitize the tumors for the Ukrain. It has caused a rash all over her body, and has caused sores in her mouth, making eating painful. She has stopped taking it for now.

Whenever we get a setback like this I'm gripped by an unreasonable cold fear. The kind that comes unbidden in the night and wraps its icy hands around my heart. It's a constant battle to push it back down into the background. It's not that I'm a stranger to fear. After all, I've been in point blank small arms fire fights. I've been in hand-to-hand combat with knives and bayonets. I've faced automatic weapons fire and have faced a variety of lethal weapons. But then I was fortunate enough to move out of the South Bronx.

Sandy and I want to thank all of you for your support, your good energy, your prayers, and your hopes for her recovery. We are aware of the odds, but she's already ahead of the curve and we fully expect to beat this thing, or at least fight it to a standstill. We wish all of you a year of love, a year of remembering to appreciate one another, and saying so to those you care about. We wish the world a year of peace and an end to the "My God is better than your God" insanity. For all its faults, we are privileged to live in a country that is among humankind's most noble experiments. Let's all count our blessings and live each day of 2007 to the fullest.

JANUARY 5, 2007

I hope you all had a terrific holiday season. We finished the year rather poorly. Around Christmas we were hoping to get Sandy another shot for the neck pain, which was getting back to unbearable. The doctor was unavailable to do it, and told her to double up her pain medication instead. Unfortunately, he didn't take her body weight, or lack thereof, into consideration. By New Year's Eve she was incoherent and hallucinating. Her breathing was very shallow and she was unable, or unwilling, to eat. She went three days with no solid food, drinking only a shake I made for her over the three days. As a result, her weight is now just under eighty-four pounds. Of the six friends who saw her in the twenty-four-hour period starting New Year's Eve, at least half thought it was the end. I had cut the pain medication in half and am doling it out to her. The stuff is slowly leaving her system and she's returning to normal. On Wednesday she felt well enough to go shopping and have lunch with Beverly Hammond (from the Mountain) and then go out to dinner with the Hammonds and Eddie and Norine Corbo (from New York). We even danced a little bit. [*It was to be the last time we danced.*] She paid for it yesterday, though, which was pretty bad, but was starting to feel better by last night, and is back to wisecracking again. We find something to laugh about every day, although some of our humor is kind of dark.

About nine or ten months before the lung diagnosis, Sandy had a squamous cell carcinoma removed from her leg. They had to dig very deep to get it all. Squamous cell carcinoma has the ability to metastasize. I believe that may have been what happened. It may help explain the tumor's extreme resistance to the chemos that have been tried. Oh yeah, in the "Really Getting Annoying" category, it turns out that I have a squamous cell carcinoma under my left eye. As our friend Boo from Madison said, "You just can't make this stuff up." At this rate we expect we'll have our own prime-time soap opera before long. Maybe we'll have a contest to come up with an appropriate name for it.

JANUARY 14, 2007

We are continuing on our emotional yo-yo. After several very bad days, we've got Sandy's medications straightened out. She still has a lot of pain, but we're controlling it as well as we can. Her CEA (cancer cell count) more than doubled a week ago over the two previous weeks. I haven't told her because I think it may be a faulty number. Yes, of course, I'm a Pollyanna, but there may be just cause. Her blood numbers (CBCs) are all in the normal range. Her appetite is good, and she's gained three pounds these last few days—a twenty-seven percent increase in her body weight. Doctor friends of ours have told me that those things wouldn't normally happen if the cancer was going so wild. We are going to have her blood drawn and sent to a different lab this coming week. She's had a couple of very good days in a row, in spite of the pain, and we even went out last night and hope to go out again tonight.

Our friends Linda and John Silvati arrive on Tuesday and will be here for a week. The day after they leave, our friends Bobby and Phyllis Ciovacco are arriving from New York, and the next day our son Alan is getting here with our grandson, Justin. We're looking forward to a terrific couple of weeks. Sandy has gained weight primarily due to the cooking of our friend Sarah's mother, Libby, who cooks up high calorie stuff that Sandy loves. She sends it over with Sarah's father, Sir Ralph (truly an inside joke, but he will forever be Sir Ralph to us. I started calling him that when I first met him). I, of course, don't eat it, as the quest for added pounds for Sandy has already cost me twenty unneeded pounds.

Many people have been urging me to call a hospice to help care for Sandy, and I've been having so much trouble with her pain management and nutrition that we had them come in and talk to us yesterday. We learned a lot of very valuable information about the things we seem to be doing right, but we also found out, among other things, that there are different kinds of meds for different kinds of pain—bone pain, visceral pain, and nerve pain—that we hadn't been told about. Sandy has been getting meds strictly to treat visceral pain, which is from the cancer, and not for nerve pain, which is in her neck and is by far the worst of it. I'm convinced that all doctors are geniuses who don't listen to anybody but themselves. We decided not to do hospice, though, because it's very much an end game deal, and we're not there yet, and hope not to be for a long, long time. So we'll kind of bop along like we've been doing and live life one day at a time and try to find things to laugh at every day. Actually, we don't have to try that hard.

JANUARY 18, 2007

We got Sandy's blood numbers yesterday. We were quite nervous because last week's cancer count numbers had spiked so unexpectedly. This week all her blood numbers were in the normal range except her hemoglobin, which is slightly low. Her CEA (cancer cell number), which is critical, dropped almost fifteen percent. It's still very, very high, but at least it's headed in the right direction again. One of the reasons that the doctor in Mississippi has such a high rate of survivorship among lung cancer patients is that he treats the immune system as well as the cancer. We felt that doing that along with the stem cell therapy for her immune system was the only real chance she had. So far, she's survived longer than about seventy percent of people who are diagnosed with this disease. The oncologists here would have us ignore the immune system, as well as everything else, like high cholesterol, and just take whatever the chemo *du jour* is. The other day one said, "We'll do whatever you want if Sandy wants to keep fighting. It's all a crap shoot anyway." Truly words to warm one's heart. That's why I say we're fighting the cancer, the pain, and the doctors too. On a truly horrible note, we got word that a very dear friend of ours from the Mountain was killed in an ice storm yesterday in Springfield, Missouri. Dave Mears had apparently pulled out of his garage early yesterday morning and had gotten out to close the garage door (no electricity) when the vehicle slid down on the ice and pinned him to the house. He will be sorely missed. It once again reminds us how fickle life is and why we should enjoy every moment and cherish all those whom we hold dear.

JANUARY 28, 2007

Sandy has deteriorated badly over the last week or so. She weighed 79 pounds this morning, which is actually up a couple of pounds. I had to take her to an emergency clinic today to get hydrated. We'll do it again tomorrow. Apparently the oncologist said it needed to be done, but we were only told to do it if we felt it was necessary. She's very weak and can barely walk or sit up without help. The trainers from the Mountain, Joey Grebenor and Meme Stabor, have a winter gig here and came up with a 2,000-calorie shake. I got her to drink most of it the last couple of days, which explains the slight weight gain, but I'm not having much luck today. Hopefully, the hydration will make her feel a bit better. Her lips are parched and her insides are boiling from the medication, which I've drastically reduced, and from the cancer. Her blood numbers keep going up. They're all in the normal range, so I feel like we're making progress against the cancer but we're fighting a whole bunch of stuff.

Our son Alan was here for a couple of days with his girlfriend [*now his wife*] Meredith Lathbury, and our five-year-old grandson, Justin. It did Sandy a lot of good to see them, although she did say about Justin at one point, "He's so LOUD!!" Our dear friends from New York, Bobby and Phyllis Ciovacco, are down here to see us, which is great. Our daughter Leah is arriving on the 5th and will stay to the 8th. Our old, old friends Al and Jane Schwartz arrive on the 9th from Santa Fe and will stay until the 13th, when Sandy's childhood friends from Texas, Linda Lee and Sami, arrive for a couple of days. Hopefully on February 1st I'll have this cancer cut out of my face so maybe we can have a family recovery ward. If I can just get Sandy to where she regains some strength, I think we can beat this thing. After all, she's got to get better so that she can take care of me because I'm fast approaching blubbering idiot status. Of course, many of you think I achieved that plateau long ago.

FEBRUARY 7, 2007

Things have been a bit rough lately. Sandy's CEA (cancer cell count) is up to 7,312, an increase of twenty-six percent in two weeks (normal is 3.0 to 10.0). The Ukrain has apparently stopped working, as all chemos do eventually. In spite of the fact that she was rehydrated with saline solution last week, Sandy remains badly dehydrated, and we'll have a nursing service come in tomorrow to do it again after I take her for a PET scan to show where the cancer is and if it's spread.

We're trying a new alterative approach since traditional medicine can offer us nothing except trial and error. Through an old friend, Skip Pierret, in Columbus, Indiana, I found a writer for medical journals who led us to a doctor in Fort Myers, Florida, whom we decided to visit. We were a bit skeptical when we walked into his office for the first time yesterday, though. Our daughter Leah was with us. The two girls behind the desk where both about six feet tall, dressed in identical tight black sweaters, black skirts, mesh stockings, and knee-length leather boots. I kept looking for the cameras. The doctor is a little guy who is sort of like the mad scientist on steroids. He has excellent credentials though, and he is going to try to determine what works on her cancer by blood tests, something nobody has yet done. He changed most of the supplements she was taking, since three of them promote cell growth, which includes cancer cells. She's so frail and dehydrated the problem is going to be keeping her alive long enough to get all the results back in ten to fourteen days. She has started to eat much better and drink more though after this guy put the fear of God in her. He finally got through to her how very serious this is. In the interim he's doing several things to kill and/or control the cancer cells. She's tough as nails and is hanging in there. Having family and friends visit from around the country keeps her spirits up. It also keeps her from complaining at me too much for making her drink, eat, and take her pills. If the tables are ever turned and I'm sick and she has to take care of me, she's going to be hell on wheels. I appeal in advance to all of you to help rescue me if that happens.

FEBRUARY 16, 2007

Sandy is doing very poorly. I'll try to send out an update tomorrow. We're going to try a new drug that has been extremely effective but it's a very convoluted process to get it and she's very weak and losing her will.

FEBRUARY 18, 2007

These last couple of weeks have not gone too well. Sandy's weight dropped to seventy-six pounds, but at least has stayed there for the last week. She's eating a bit more and drinking a lot of water. I keep making her high calorie shakes, but it takes her a few days to drink most of one. Last week our sons Matthew and Mark were here. Our very old friends from New York, and now of Santa Fe, Al and Jane Schwartz, were here at the same time as Matt and Mark, and among them all they had Sandy laughing all weekend. Jane cooked and froze seventeen meals for us. Amazing.

Sandy's childhood friends, Linda Lee Dupnik and Sami Shirley, arrived from Aransas Pass, Texas, the day Al and Jane left and Linda Lee cooked a bunch of Texican stuff for her so she's eating food she loves, a little bit at a time. The other day I was talking to her about how lucky we are to have so many incredible friends and how she has touched the lives of hundreds of people in more than forty states. She said it was because she threatened to kill them all. Linda and John Silvati arrive from Cincinnati tonight for the third time in three months. Our friends from Texas, Scooter and Gail Reasor, are driving over from Miami this afternoon to bring Sandy stone crabs from Joe's Stone Crab, one of her favorite things in the world.

For the last seven weeks several people have told me she was going to die, that she was near death, and I need to "give her permission." I don't know why. She never needed my permission for anything else. I know she's in a lot of pain and sometimes has said she just wants it to be over. In the meantime, she went for a manicure and pedicure last week, talks about going to a spa, and is anxious to get back to the Mountain where she wants to write a book about all this. We originally thought her cough was due to the fact that she's allergic to our cat, Cleocatra. As a result she wants to call the book, *Maybe It's a Hairball*. The oncologist has said that everything we've done is sane and logical and that whenever one door closes another door opens. In that vein, Howell Hammond from the Mountain, who, along with his wife Beverly (known to her friends as the Mother of the World) have been beyond incredible. They found out about a drug that, just this past Tuesday, stopped clinical trials and became available due to its amazing success against cancer, particularly in the liver. It's a convoluted process but we should have Sandy on it shortly, along with chemos that will start this week to which her tumor has shown susceptibility. I know it's selfish on my part but I keep asking her for one more day, and as long as she keeps giving this to me we've got a shot.

[*Beverly Hammond has asked to be described in this book as a tall, slender blonde. So this is for you, Beverly—Beverly Hammond, the tall, slender blonde, is a remarkable woman and a truly amazing friend.*]

MARCH 9, 2007

We started a new treatment yesterday: low-dose chemo that has no side effects, and massive doses of vitamin C. We're doing this with the doctor in Fort Myers, who, although strange, has exemplary credentials. We also found out he's married to one of the six-foot-tall girls in his office. This conjures up mental images I'm striving mightily to put out of my head. I truly have to poke out my mind's eye. This guy's even shorter than I am. He could probably walk under a table and not bump his head. We're hoping that this treatment will reverse the growth of the cancer, particularly in Sandy's liver, where it currently presents the most danger. If her liver and heart hold out, I think we've got a real shot. She's down to only seventy pounds and is, of course, very weak. She needs help to get herself into a sitting position, to stand up, and to walk. She's most comfortable lying down. She eats very small amounts but exists on the shakes I make her every day. They provide about 1,400 calories or so—plenty for her weight —a ton of vitamins and minerals, and antioxidants. Her cancer cell count went up about six percent in the last month. That's actually OK. For one thing, up to ten percent either way is negligible. For the last month we've done nothing except the shakes with the antioxidants, so my theory is that her immune system has kind of stabilized itself.

We also finally got this new drug, Nexavar, two days ago, after a month of fighting, so she has started on that also. It has severe side effects in thirty percent of the cases, though, so I have to watch her closely. Her oncologist grants us an audience once a month, except he's too busy this month. With certain notable exceptions I've lost all respect for the medical profession. I knew about the vitamin C potential for a while, but was trying other things. I should have tried it sooner. Many of our Mountain friends are gathering in Sarasota this weekend for the annual Mountain Air South Golf, Eating and Drinking Tournament. Since Sandy and I are on injured reserve and can't attend they're saving quite a bit on the drinking portion. We sorely miss going because it's one of the great weekends of the year, but it'll make it even more fun for us when we're there next year and win the golf tournament. I actually got to play golf the other day with a group of Mountain friends and, as I mentioned on the course, it was nice to find out that playing so rarely the last couple of years hasn't affected my game in the slightest.

MARCH 12, 2007

Last Wednesday evening we finally got the Nexavar after a month of trying and started Sandy on it. On Thursday she had her first doses of low-dose chemo and massive doses of vitamin C. She took a pain pill Friday morning, as she's done every day since March 1, 2006, when she had the neck vertebrae fusion operation and has been in constant pain since. Starting Friday afternoon, she no longer wanted the pain pills and has not needed them since. She was doing fine until about 4:30 A.M. Sunday morning when she started to experience some shortness of breath and had some bleeding. We stopped the Nexavar, as these are listed as possible side effects. By 4:30 A.M. yesterday morning (Monday) she was hallucinating. She thought we were in a trailer and were moving. I doubt that Sandy's ever been in a trailer in her life, so this was truly a hallucination. By late morning she couldn't even walk with assistance and became non-responsive. I called 911 and took her to the hospital by ambulance. Howell and Beverly Hammond followed us down there and stayed until almost 10:00 P.M., when we left Sandy resting comfortably. Boo Mortenson came down also, and Linda Silvati is flying in today from Cincinnati. Sandy said to Linda about a month ago, "I'm not afraid of dying. I'm just disappointed."Through Mountain friends, John and Paulette Kempfer, who have an association with this hospital, Sandy has a room on the top floor in a special section with a view of the Gulf. The doctors all use the same words, telling me after they've pulled me aside, "She's a sick puppy." Obviously I know that. Maybe I should have taken her to a veterinarian for all the good these guys are doing her. The oncologist told me to stop the Nexavar for a while and when we continue it we'll reduce the dosage.

Sandy will be in the hospital for a couple of days,

get hydrated, and hopefully be in good enough condition to continue her treatments. I still think we can beat the cancer. It's all the other stuff that scares me. I know I haven't conveyed the terror I've felt, nor have I tried, because there's no way to describe it. I just keep believing, and try to keep Sandy believing, that we'll get through this too, as long as she keeps giving me one more day, and never, ever quits.

MARCH 14, 2007

This will be brief. I just came home from the hospital to shower and change and am on my way back. Sandy is having trouble breathing and her liver is infused with cancer. It's also in both lungs and her back. Barring extraordinary measures—like a feeding tube, which she has refused, or a Miracle—it's unlikely she can make it back home. If the worst happens, I'll take her back to Pound Ridge, New York, where we spent our seventeen happiest years. We have a beautiful plot on a hillside beneath a stone wall that we've had for years. If that happens, please, no flowers. Make any donations in Sandy's name to our favorite charity, Save The Children, 54 Wilton Road, Westport, CT 06880, Attn: Marie Orsini Rosen. I'm not giving up yet, though, but I'm more frightened than I've ever been in my life. Still, I'm the only one who thinks there's a chance. If she can make it out of the hospital and resume treatment, vitamin C, etc., we've got a shot, but it's not looking good at the moment. Thank you all for your unflagging belief, hope, and support. Lung cancer is the most deadly form of cancer for women, in that it kills more women each year than even breast cancer. The great majority of lung cancer patients die within six to nine months of diagnosis. Next week will be twenty-one months for Sandy. She's the strongest person I ever met. On some level I was in love with her long before I met her. No matter what happens, I will be in love with her until the end of time.

MARCH 15, 2007

As all of you know from our son Mark's e-mail this morning, at 8:35 A.M., while I was with her, the light went out of my life forever. So ends a tale of struggle, courage, pain, laughter, hope, and most of all, amazing happiness and love. Thank you all for all that you've done for us. Those near and far, we felt your love and support every step of the way. Sandy and I both thank all of you from the bottom of our hearts.

MARCH 25, 2007

We buried Sandy on March 19th. The day before, the 18th, was twenty-four years and seven months from the day we met, in a location not far from where she now rests. The funeral service was not a service at all, just those who wanted to get up and say what they felt. Since it involved Sandy, it was lively and very funny and there was a great deal of laughter mingled with the tears. There were almost fifty people there. They came from as far away as New Mexico, Indiana, Virginia, Ohio, Pennsylvania, Maryland, New Jersey, and, of course, our home states of New York, North Carolina, Florida, and Texas. At the cemetery I told the story of the day we picked out the plots. It was a beautiful fall day with multicolored leaves on the trees and on the ground. We had a list of the available plots, and as we went around to see them I would lie down in each one to check the view. We picked the best available view, with a stone wall at our heads and a lovely view of a preserve down the hill. I was told Neil Simon will be in the same row, just a few spots away, so the conversation should be as good as the view.

I mentioned at the service that I would write a book for Sandy (this book), and it would be called *Champagne and Roses* because that's what our life together was. It was a fairy tale that just didn't have "a happily ever after" long enough, although no amount of time would have been long enough. I also said that one of our greatest joys was to have our friends meet our friends, and that even now, at the end, we were still doing just that. She would have loved it. So, if any of you find yourself in the lovely hamlet of Pound Ridge, New York, go to the cemetery, find our stone wall, and visit Sandy. She'll smile knowing that you're there. And if, by chance, while you're there you feel a slight breeze, a whisper of air on your cheek, a ray of sunshine in your hair, it's Sandy greeting you, happy that you're there. My Sandy, my love till the end of time.

Chapter 4

Letters from the Heart

OVER THE COURSE of Sandy's illness, we were buoyed by a continuous stream of letters and e-mails from our friends and family, all encouraging Sandy and wishing her a speedy recovery. The full collection of these is too numerous to include in the book. What I felt was particularly touching, and which I wanted to share, were the condolence notes and letters I received shortly before, and right after Sandy died. These were so, so special to me. To this day they still remind me of how much Sandy was loved by so many. I have included many of them here. I thank everyone for allowing me to share them.

From Late 2006 and Early 2007

Dearest Art and Sandy,

So touched by your words! I am gripped by both of you. Your courage and love have taken you through a most unbelievable passage in life. This was not in the plans nor invited into your lives, yet you both are conquerors of ever getting done in, washed up, lacking in spirit, but just keeping your hearts close to home and persevering against all odds that have often been unfair and unjust. We celebrate you both as huge warriors and conquerors that know no defeat!!! Thank God for people like you.

Your good words will always be with us, and yes, we share your thoughts as well. Through you both we have an even greater appreciation for all that is in our lives and not to take anything for granted. It can all change and, most importantly, it's just one beautiful day at a time. Hugs and words to those we love are all-important.

We love you both, and even though we have not seen you since our trip, you remain in our hearts and souls forever. You are good people, and we are privileged to know you.

Thank you for letting us into your lives. May God bless you—whatever god he is!!!

—Barb and Mo Novikoff, Poway, California

We met Barb and Mo, along with several other couples who appear in this book, on a trip we took around the world in September 2003.

You are right to keep the faith. I am continuing my St. Jude prayer, and have great hopes for 2007. It is very hard to think of Sandy in such pain, but rash and all, I'm sure she is still one of the best looking women on the planet. As with you, we wish all, especially, you and Sandy, a year of hopes realized and dreams come true. We love you both. We never stop thinking of you and Sandy with good thoughts.

Love always,
Bob and Phillis Ciovacco

I have known Bobby and Phyllis since we were teen-
agers. Bobby and I shared a fire escape. He is also my
attorney.

~

Dear Art,

I am sure you get so many emails…but I wanted to tell you
that I pray for both of you every day…actually more than that.
Tonight on the news the reporters were mentioning how devoted
a couple the Fords had been. Well, they didn't have anything on
you and Sandy! The way you two are, well, I haven't seen it many
times. I know there are many couples who deeply love each other,
but you two…glow and sparkle. I am so sorry you two are having
such a challenging time. Damn. I can't think of one good thing
to say about that.

But know you both are in our hearts and thoughts…always.

Fondly,

Karen and Bob Miller, Mountain Air, North Carolina

~

Arty and Sandy,

It's Jordan Schwartz. I hope you don't mind my reading the
e-mail you sent to Dad and Jane. I have been so sorry to hear
about what has happened, and my parents have been keeping me
informed about Sandy's condition.

I must say that there is no other couple in the world who would
have the moxy to create and continue an e-mail chain to keep
everyone who knows and loves them so honestly apprised of what

is going on. I admire your strength and your ability to find the humor in even the most difficult times.

It came as no surprise to me to read that the very moment Sandy felt even a little better she was shopping, socializing, and dancing. This is the way I think of you both. The ultimate hosts and entertainers. I often think of the time we were away together in Boca Raton (how glamorous Sandy looked in her sparkling evening gowns) and how much I looked forward to when we would visit in Pound Ridge. I will never forget how you two came to see us after my mom passed away. You had been away when you heard the news. My mother did not have many close friends in her life. You were two of her closest. I remember hearing about your trips to New Orleáns—Sandy and mom shopping day after day and having the best time, spending a fortune, but always coming home with at least four or five new pairs of shoes.

I am thinking of you both and am in complete admiration of your strength, love of life and each other.

All my love,
Jordan

Jordan is the daughter of my friend, Al Schwartz, whom I refer to as my oldest living friend (not time, but age) and his late wife, Leslie. Al is from New York City. He and Jane currently live in Santa Fe, New Mexico. Jordan was married in Santa Fe in October 2008 to a terrific young man named Erik Hendin. They live in New York where she has a company called Chefs in the City.

Hi guys,

We have to thank you for your e-mails and updates. It's the only way we know that our prayers are still being answered. Art, I don't know if you were a writer in your earlier years, but you have quite a gift with words and humor. We look forward to your e-mails more than most books we are reading.

I don't know if you have looked into acupuncture for Sandy, but with the right doctor (I know that is the key to everything) Sandy may be able to get some relief from that neck/nerve pain without medication. Personally, I believe one hundred percent in acupuncture treatments (as I do stem cell). I'm sure the thought of needles in her neck is not a comforting one, but the treatment has been around for over one hundred years and insurance is now covering treatments which was almost unheard of ten years or so ago. If you put it out there to your network of friends (see, I'm looking for another e-mail) I'll bet your response will be better than the stem cell stories.

We may be coming over to Naples on the 25th for one night (it's John Toussel's b'day and he's wild right now because New Orleans won yesterday and he was at the game) and we would love to stop and say hi if you don't have too much company, but if you do, that's ok because we'll be back in another couple of weeks. You inspire Ralph and I in our marriage. Thank you both for that, this is what it's all about.

Love to both of you,
Debbie and Ralph, Mountain Air

Ralph and Debbie Muller from the Mountain. We had tried acupuncture. It gave her some relief but only for a couple of hours at a time. We did it often.

Art,

I can't take you on my plane, or boat, or private island. I can only take you back to thirty years of fighting the good fight, the tears, the laughs and the camaraderie.

You and Sandy have been in my life and in my heart from day one. I can only hope my being with you both will bring a smile to your lips and the support of my love.

Your oldest living friend,
Al Schwartz, Santa Fe, New Mexico

I am sure I told you that I always pass these on to my dad as I am sure they are intended for him, BUT I read every one of them. You both are a true inspiration to all. Your efforts and heart boggle my mind. KEEP IT UP! Can't wait for the e-mail that says Sandy is 150 lbs and running circles around you!

Bill Pierro Jr., LC, New York, New York

Tell her she has come this far and has tons of support teams cheering her on. We will not take "no will" at this time. I know this is easy for me to say, but we must get our boots on and let Sandy know we want her to be in the world and not to let anything stand in her way. God knows the pain she has been through and you as her strongest, most incredible man who adores her with every inch of his body and will. God must take this all under account. I know you don't believe in a formal guy up there; but hell, at this point *if anyone is listening just give Sandy a chance.*

Our love,
Barb and Mo Novikoff, Poway, Calfornia

⟜

I agree. Let's take this day by day. As we have seen with Howell, new things are happening all the time. There are literally more people than we can count who, through various means—not the least of which is prayer—want to reverse this situation because we love you both and we know how much you love each other. The cumulative weight of all this love and friendship, I believe, will not go for naught. I look forward to Sandy's smooth and sexy voice on karaoke night on the Mountain and her book. As long as she's in the fight, we're with her. We believe that sometimes things don't go right for a long time, but if you stay in the fight, things can change dramatically for the good. That's what we, along with all your friends, are hoping will happen. As bad as it has been, that's as good as we hope it will get. We're here if you need us. We're praying for you. We're praying for you constantly.

All our love.
Beverly and Howell Hammond, Mountain Air, North Carolina

⟜

Dear Art,
I am in awe of both you and Sandy as you continue the fight. Art, you are the "gold standard" in loving, hopeful support while still maintaining your sense of humor—and, I might add, New York cynicism—especially as it relates to the medical profession. As Chair of one of the ten largest health care systems in the

country I have taken your experiences back to Indiana and asked the tough questions your experiences raise. The health care system is an anachronism. It is unaccepting of process or technology, and heaven forbid that a doctor would treat a patient as a customer.

Keep fighting and loving that lil' Texan who I will always envision, even though I never saw her as such, as the featured twirler for the Hurricane band.

Love from the Hunts.
Bill and Nancy, Indianapolis, Indiana

Bill and Nancy are friends from the Around the World trip in 2003.

Dear Art,

We are so sorry that this is happening to our Sandy, one of the brightest stars on our planet. What a courageous woman and fighter she has been. She has set a wonderful example of bravery in the face of adversity, and has set a high bar for all of us to follow. May God give you peace with the knowledge that she is staying with us as long as she can and that you are married to one of the greatest women of all time.

Much love,
Denise and Wild Bill Stealey, Mountain Air, North Carolina

Condolence Letters Upon the Passing of Sandy

The light went out of your life, but the light will never go out. I am so sorry for the pain you are feeling, my friend. There is nothing I (or anyone) can do but keep you in our prayers.

She was an amazing woman, one of a kind, and you were both so fortunate to have found each other. I always thought it was a fairy tale romance.

Nanci Gibbs, Durham, North Carolina

~

Dear Art:

Marie Orsini Rosen immediately notified me of Sandy's passing this morning. You and Sandy have been part of Save the Children's family for nearly fifteen years, and during that time, you and she have generously and unselfishly found many ways to support our work with girls and boys in need.

Now it is our turn to offer our support to you. Please know that you and your family are in our thoughts at this heartbreaking time. You may recall that I met you and Sandy some years ago when you visited Save the Children with your sponsored child, Lance, and his mother. Meeting you then and knowing you now, I am moved and grateful, but not surprised, that you have asked your and Sandy's families and friends to honor her memory with contributions to our work with children. Her beautiful legacy will live on in the Children's future.

On behalf of my colleagues and the children whose lives you and Sandy have touched all these years, please accept my condolences.

Sincerely,
Charlie MacCormack
President and CEO, Save the Children

~

Sandy and I on a cruise with our dear friends Al and Jane
Schwartz, New Year's Eve, 1992.

At Sandy's surprise 60th birthday party on the Mountain
June 16, 2000.

At her surprise 60th. That's Phyllis Ciovacco in the corner and
Gloria and Jimmy Peer on the right.

Part of her 4 day, 3 night surprise 60th birthday celebration on the Mountain.

Also at her surprise 60th. I threw surprise parties for her on her 50th in Pound Ridge, New York, her 55th, in Corpus Christi, Texas, her 60th and her 65th on the Mountain in North Carolina. She never got it. I would have sold my soul to have been able to throw a 70th surprise birthday party for her.

New Year's Eve, 2004 at the home of our friends from Texas,
Scooter and Gail Reaser at their home in Santa Fe, New Mexico.
It was to be our last great New Year's Eve. We found out
about the cancer six months later.

Sandy, me and our two Whippets, B.B. the white one, and
Gabriella, the little brindle one who died in Sandy's arms rushing
to the emergency Vet in Asheville, North Carolina the night that
Sandy was diagnosed with cancer. Gabby was 10. B.B. died New
Year's eve, 2007, 9 and a half months after Sandy died. He was 15.

At the Kentucky Derby May 5, 2006 10 months before she
died. She was already quite sick at that time. This picture
was taken by Jerry Raemisch of Madison, Wisconsin.
Tragically his wife, Linda, died of cancer the day
we were burying Sandy.

Sandy and I at a party we threw at our home in Naples, Florida, February 4, 2006. This picture was taken by our friend Dottie LLoyd. 13 months later I would bury her in this outfit.

Oh, Arthur,

May you find
comfort
in the familiar embrace
of family,
strength
in the caring hearts
of friends,
and peace
in the healing power
of time.

Our sincerest and heart-
felt condolences!

Judy and Bob

We are glad she is out of pain,
but sorry that there wasn't
another way.

We are so happy the two of you
found each other but sorry
you didn't get at least 20 more
years.

We are grateful that you
created so many wonderful
memories

But sorry you will be
lost in your loss
for awhile.

We hope our friendship
will continue to last
but will forever miss
"our sunshine"!

Love to you, Arthur,
S.

Card from Judy and Bob Black, Kingwood, Texas, shortly after Sandy died.

Champagne and Roses
Forever

ARTHUR JAY BENSON
SEPTEMBER 3, 1939
BRONX, NEW YORK

SANDRA SUE BENSON
JUNE 16, 1940
ARANSAS PASS, TEXAS
MARCH 15, 2007
NAPLES, FLORIDA

Our headstone. Pound Ridge Town Cemetery, New York.

She fought the good fight exceptionally well. She beat the odds for longer than could be expected. She was a fighter and a lover! Her life here on Earth is past, but her memory will live on with all of us.

Art, you fought the good fight exceptionally well. You set the curve on loving support. Your life here on earth is not past. Sandy would want you to grab for the gusto in due time. Remember that the best thing you can do for her is to take care of yourself. As hard as it will be in the near term, you have a long and joyful life ahead of you. There will always be emptiness, but remember how Sandy would want you to live your life—to the max!

Love to a great guy,
Bill and Nancy Hunt, Indianapolis, Indiana

Dearest Art,

Thank you for the privilege of having shared some of that struggle, courage, pain, laughter, hope, amazing apiñes, and love. Your love for each other and life, your devotion, and Sandy's strength and spirit are something we will always rejoice in. We are grateful to know you, and will be holding you close, as we will Sandy, always.

This morning, I woke a few minutes before 6:00 A.M. which was 9:00 A.M. your time. This is very unusual for me, as I'm a sleeper (yesterday Bill had to shake me at 8:30 A.M.). I had been restless, and a bird woke me up easily. This bird had a very distinctive call—exuberant, I'd say. I'd like to say that if I'd seen the bird she would have had a fabulous smile with a bright beak, shapely figure, and drop-dead gorgeous feathers. I think it might have been Sandy just passing through on her way to the paradise she deserves.

We love you, Art.
Susy Entriger, Scottsdale, Arizona

Susy and Bill Entriger are our friends from the Around the World trip.

～

Dearest Art,

My heart, my prayers and my sympathy go out to you during this very difficult time. I know that the past twenty-one months have all been difficult as you and Sandy fought this terrible monster that is cancer. I have to tell you how honored I have felt to have been able to share this courageous journey with you and Sandy through your many e-mails (I have saved every one). I know Sandy knew how lucky she was to have you as her husband and advocate throughout her illness. You were relentless in persuing treatments and options, leaving no stone unturned, and we have all learned from your determination. Although the Bensons and the Hunts really have not spent much time together, I have felt such a part of your heart and your journey through your letters in which you shared your ups and downs, your successes and frustrations.

You and Sandy had a very special love for each other, and I know that the pain you are experiencing now must feel devastating. I cannot find the words to comfort, except to let you know that we all weep for your loss and send our most loving prayers that you will be held close during the months to come, as you turn your attention away from doctors and treatments and caretaking and begin to take care of yourself. I know that you have many friends and I hope you let them hold you up during this time, surrounding you with love and hugs and shoulders to cry on and opportunities to tell your story over and over and over.

It was such fun getting to know you on our Around the World adventure. What a fun couple! I remember all of Sandy's wonderful clothes and hats and your comments that she had all the suitcases filled with her things, leaving you with very little space for your own things. It was a good thing that you could add that great sarong to your wardrobe in the Maldives. I smile when I remember her enthusiasm, her sense of humor, her love for you...I can hear her as clear as day saying your name so lovingly, "Arthur...."

I know it may be a while before you are in touch again, but I want to let you know that we are here and that we care and want to know how you are doing. I think you should write a book; you have much to teach! Perhaps we should just bind all of your e-mails. Bill and I lift our glasses to you and to Sandy and to your wonderful but all-too-brief life together!

Love,

Nancy Hunt

~

Art,

Karen and I want to extend our deepest condolences on Sandy's passing. You and Sandy were one of the earliest folks we met when we first came to the Mountain, and Sandy was among the main reasons why we love the Mountain as much as we do. We want you to know our thoughts, prayers and love will be with you and your family.

Your love and devotion for Sandy will go down as one of the greatest love stories of all time. Sandy reflected the personality, friendship, and love we at Mountain Air strive to have.

We will not be able to attend the services early next week due to Karen's mother also being ill, but our thoughts will be with you.

God bless you and Sandy.

Lonny

Warshaw, Mountain Air, North Carolina

Arthur,

I wish I could find words adequate for what I want to say, but they just don't seem to be enough. I want you to know, though, that when I think of you and Sandy, the first thing that pops into my head is the tremendous love you had for each other. It is so rare to observe and even rarer to experience. I feel that it has to make the pain deeper..., but oh, what a joy to have known it. To have been so fortunate to have found each other. . .and recognized it. . .and shared part of your lives together. Please know that she was a light in all of our lives, and will be truly missed. We are with you in thought and prayers and hope that your knowing this will be of some comfort.

We love you,

Judy and Chuck Ruhman, Aransas Pass, Texas

Judy and Chuck are friends from Sandy's hometown.

Although we were the newest of friends, Sandy touched me in the most beautiful way. I felt as if I had known her all my life.

We just seemed to connect as soon as we met! I feel as if my life has been enriched by being touched by this amazing woman—her brilliance, her laughter, her intelligence, her fun-loving spirit. I enjoyed our ever-too-short time together and Sandy will always have a special place in my heart. She was an exceptional person and friend! I am so sorry for your loss. I know that the two of you have many beautiful memories that will forever burn brightly in your mind and heart. You will keep her alive within you forever, and her friends will keep her alive within themselves. She will be sorely missed and forever loved.

If there is anything I can do to help you in any way, especially down here, please let me know. Otherwise, as you lay the light of your life to rest, remember you shared a deep love that will last forever until you meet again.

You and your family are in our thoughts and prayers. I will miss my "girlfriend"!

Dottie Lloyd, Naples, Florida

Dottie and Mike Lloyd were our new friends from Florida.

It is a sad week for Mountain Air. It is with great sadness that we announce the passing of Sandra "Sandy" Benson on Thursday, March 15, following a courageous battle with cancer. The Bensons are at their home in Naples, Florida.

Art and Sandy have been part of the Mountain Air family since December 1, 1998, and are active members of the Club. Sandy was much loved by the entire Mountain Air family. She and Art, seemingly inseparable, served as a true inspiration to all of us through their display of courage and kindness.

Our heartfelt condolences and prayers go out to Art and his family.

In lieu of flowers, Art has requested that those who wish to make a donation do so to their favorite charity, Save The Children, 54 Wilton Road, Westport, CT 06880, Attn: Marie Orsim Rosen.

Marilyn Robinson
Membership Sales and Services, Mountain Air, North Carolina

❧

We received the e-mail from you, Art, that we prayed we would never see, the one you hoped beyond hope that you wouldn't have to write, the one that for so long it seemed you wouldn't have to write. Please accept our most deepest sympathy. Your words touched us to the core. Your Sandy has to be the most incredible woman ever to grace this earth. Please try to take care of yourself and let your family wrap you in their love and caring. Thank you again for keeping us informed and thanks to your wonderful son for writing to all of us. We will keep in touch with you and may you be able to find some comfort in all of your wonderful memories.

With love,
Lauren and Arnie Green, Boca Raton, Florida

Lauren and Arnie were our new friends from Florida.

❧

Art:

The picture of Sandy lying on the couch weighing virtually nothing will be in my mind forever. I know that you did everything that you could possibly do, physically, monetarily, and mentally. Sometimes no matter how hard you try you can't alter the outcome. I am proud you are my friend. I am sorry.

Bob Ciovacco, Sea Cliff, New York

Dear Art,

Our deepest heartfelt condolences on the loss of Sandy. We know your heart is broken. She was such a delightful person and I had a lot of fun with her, especially on karaoke nights singing "Hotel California." She was a hoot. She loved and enjoyed life to the fullest. God bless you for all you did for her in trying to find a cure and standing by her so close till the end. She did outlive most with your tender loving care. My sister only lasted twelve months with lung cancer (non-smoker). My brother is going on sixteen months (smoker).

Your letters were funny, heartfelt and very touching. Maybe you should write a book? Sandy will be greatly missed. You and your family are in our prayers.

Sincerely,
John and Rose Gordon, Burnsville, North Carolina

John and Rose are friends from the Mountain.

I will keep both you and Sandy in my prayers. I am sorry that we couldn't help her!! What a wonderful person. At least now there is no pain and suffering, only joy for her. I know that it will not be easy to continue, but you have a great deal to offer a lot of people. Your dry since of humor takes the edge off of many situations, and I think you are sincerely a breath of fresh air!!

If I can help with anything, you know where to find me!

Wilson Galliard
Administrator for the Cancer Center in Greenwood, Mississippi

Gary and I are trying to find the words to express how sad we are and how we can comfort you. There are none. We have been talking about the fun times with the two of you and when Sandra was a freshman in high school and I was a senior. I remember her as a twirler and how good she was, how she always lit up a room when she came in, how quick she learned and preformed in tap class, our girls trip to Mexico, and on and on. We considered you all good friends and always looked forward to seeing you when you came to South Texas. Your days and nights will be hard, but you did everything humanly possible to make her well, and we admire you for it. Even though we cannot be with you to give you a hug, we hope you can continue to be strong.

Love,
Darlene and Gary Boehnke, Aransas Pass, Texas

Tragically, Gary got cancer a few months later and died in January, 2008.

Today, you have been in our hearts. It is such a sad day for all of us. What a great loss for each of us. Sandy will be forever remembered and leaves a legacy of loving friends, family and a devoted husband. Art, you are truly amazing and we will treasure your friendship forever. We are in California and sorry we cannot be with you. We are there in spirit and love.

With deepest sympathy,
Joel and Kay Levy of Rockport and Houston, Texas

Dear Art and Mark:

What a beautiful service for Sandy yesterday. I laughed and I cried, and I saw others did, too. The reaction from all of us gathered in the room was a testimony to the people she so deeply touched.

It was a privilege to be with you and your loved ones yesterday. The photograph of Sandy is how I will remember her.

Warmest regards,
Marie Orsini Rosen
Save the Children
Westport, Connecticut

Art,

The light of your life has moved on to a better place. I can't begin to tell you my sorrow at your great loss.

Peter Borges, Los Angeles, California

Peter and Vera Borges. Peter is an old friend I met in

business.

⌒

Hi Art,

My heart aches for you and your family. Sandy was so loved by so many people and always will be. I am sending all of my strength to help you become at peace with her passing. I always think heaven must be so very special with all the wonderful people there. All of us that knew you and Sandy always marvel at how much you loved each other. It was fun just watching you together. That is a very special, everlasting love. Please know that my thoughts and prayers are with you, Art.

My deepest sympathy,
Nancy Rogers, Mountain Air, North Carolina

⌒

Art:

God didn't promise days without pain, laughter without sorrow, sun without rain. But he did promise strength for the day, comfort for the tears, and light for the way.

Follow the light, my friend,
Al Schwartz, Santa Fe, New Mexico

⌒

Dear Mr. Benson:

Please accept my sincere condolences on Sandy's passing. I was so sorry to hear about Sandy on arrival back to work. As expected as this may have been, one is never prepared for the actuality. You were there with Sandy as a constant and you did all you could. I am certain kind words are wonderful in a time of need but I know they cannot fill an emptiness you must feel.

We all are saddened by this. You have both been wonderful to Save The Children.

Sincere Condolences,
Nancy A. Fekete
Coordinator, Donor Services, Save the Children

~

Dear Art,

I am sorry that I did not attend the funeral. I was in Tennessee attending another funeral—that of my friend the Navy pilot who was killed in a car crash. I think the only reason Sandy lasted as long as she did was from the enormous effort that you made. It must be extremely difficult to be doing everything possible and knowing deep down that there is nothing that you can do. I am really sorry.

Bob McArthy, Rockport, Texas

Bob and Beverly McArthy are friends from Texas.

~

I am so sorry about Sandra and have been trying to think of something to tell you that will help, but I can only tell you that you have to take one day at a time. You must remember all the wonderful times you had together and think of those. You have three grandchildren, Justin, Sophia, and Jack and you have to go on with each day because of them. It's not easy, but

*you can do it. Thank you for all the e-mails about her and you
will continue to be in my thoughts and prayers.*

Judy Meyer, Rockport, Texas.

Judy's husband, Joe Ed, died a few years earlier of
cancer. They were childhood friends of Sandy's from
Aransas Pass, Texas.

⌒

Dear Art,

*The loss of anyone as dear as Sandy tears a hole in the heart
that only time can heal. The hard part is doing the time.*

*You have my deepest sympathy. I tried to tell you last summer,
when we played golf together on the Mountain, that I think you
and Sandy made the world a better place. Now that Sandy's light
has gone out, I want you to know that I feel the world is still a
better place because Sandy was in it.*

*Thank you for all the notes you sent, sharing with us your
struggle against this terrible disease, cancer. I read each one and
have kept them all in a special folder named "Sandy's Story." I also
shared them with several friends who had cancer or had someone in
their family with the disease. Without fail, every one of them said
the notes made them feel as though they knew Sandy and they all
shed a tear when they heard the battle was lost.*

There will always be things to do and promises to keep.

Take care of yourself,
Hank Thomas, Rockport, Texas

⌒

Dear Art,

Our sincerest condolences to our loss of Sandy. She will be part of mine and Alex's lives forever. We have been talking about her beautiful face, big heart, collections of wigs, beautiful voice, her laughter and, most of all, your love for each other. She is now resting and will be waiting for all of us. We'll get together again someday and do karaoke in heaven.

Love, and take care of yourself. Our health and friends are our wealth.

Glo Campbell, Mountain Air, North Carolina
Gloria and Alex Campbell.

Dear Art,

We are engulfed with sorrow for you and beloved Sandy. We were fortunate enough to have known her for a short period of time, during which she brought many moments of laughter and fun into our lives. You are very lucky to have had her all those years—although they don't seem ever enough, but they were many great ones. She, too, was very lucky to have had such a loving and caring husband by her side during all the good times and also the bad ones. At this time there are not many words we can offer to comfort you in your distress; however, we wanted to extend our most sincere condolences at this time of loneliness and heartbreak. We are looking forward to seeing you again soon.

Your friends that care for and love you,
Susanna and Doug Totura, Mountain Air, North Carolina

Dear Artie,

Thank you so much for your update. As always you have something uplifting to say.

I know your days are long and lonely, but time has a way of eventually making things easier.

As you return to the Mountain, I will still be glad to make you some soup and our door is always open and there will be room at our table for you. Hang in there, my friend. We will see you soon.

Fondly,

Yvonne and Marv Towery, Mountain Air, North Carolina

May Sandy rest in peace and know she was loved by all who knew her, met her, and got to enjoy her spirit of life. We were there in spirit with her during that day of the funeral. What can one say at a time like this except that it was a story of "Champagne and Roses" and shall continue to be when you write that book. I have saved most of your e-mails to us because they were so inspirational, loving, hysterical, and always filled with your incredible sense of humor. Nothing got you down! Well, I know it did, but you fought the battle and I could see you pushing that big ball up the hill even when it didn't want to go uphill. You are both amazing people and it has been a privilege to know you both.

Sandy, if you are reading this with Art, just don't worry about him, he has so many good friends that will take him under their wings and keep him from feeling his missing heart. He will be there with you 'til the end of time and we will never forget your love story. It is treasured in our soul and fills our memory of just how sweet life is when you meet that one very special person who is your soul mate. Mo calls it "love of my life." We embrace all of this with you and celebrate you, Sandy, and your Art for being so generous to share this part of your life with us.

All our love, and you know our home is always open to you anytime. Sandy would have loved our guest suite. It's just an invitation whenever you find your way over here. Keep us posted on how you are doing and what you are doing, please. Do not stop your e-mails. They really have meant a lot to us.

Barb & Mo and Novikoff, Poway, California

I wish it had been possible for me to be there, and I felt an emptiness that I was not in a position to say a proper good-bye to Sandy. I can assure you that at some point I will find my way to Pound Ridge to visit her. I know in all that sorrow many had stories to share that inserted some lightness into the good-byes on Monday. Anyone who ever spent any time with Sandy will always remember her because she had a dramatic personality. I am so glad I was able to see her in January.

Even though I know you will never fully recover from this, your friends (and you have more than anyone I know) will certainly continue to support you.

Nanci Gibbs

Nanci worked for my company for many years. She and Sandy had many fun times together.

Art,

I don't know if your mention of writing a book was poetic or a statement of fact, but you certainly should. You definitely have the talent...but then you are expressing the love in your Heart...and you have the willingness to share.

Mary and Don Corcelli, Mountain Air, North Carolina

~

You and Sandy were indeed lucky to have had so many years with each other whom you loved so deeply and had such a happy relationship and life together. It was too short, but thank God you had it.

We send our love,
Dick and Daryle Prager and Family, Miami Beach, Florida

Dick and Daryle are my cousins. Daryle is a very gifted artist. She and Dick have a travel agency.

~

Art,

I think your love for each other will go beyond time.

We're thinking of both of you,
Karen and Bob Miller, Mountain Air, North Carolina

~

Hi Art,

This is from my friend in Mississippi who helped refer you to the stem cell program. I only wish we could have helped you sooner.

There is a card in the mail to you, but I'm sure you are over-whelmed with cards.

Hope to see you soon.

Love,
Debbie and Ralph Muller, Mountain Air, North Carolina

～

Dear Arthur,

Sonny and I received copies of your updates on Sandy through an old friend, Sandra LaBaume, in Corpus Christi. I shared them with friends here in Rockport, San Antonio, and Houston, all of whom were privileged to know Sandy. I can't begin to tell you how honored we were to read about your feelings and anxieties during her illness. Although no one can possibly imagine what you both were going through, your sharing of those thoughts meant so much. Thank you. When you decide to come to Rockport for a visit, please let us know. We would love to see you. We will keep you and yours in our prayers each day.

Love,
Jacque Park, Rockport, Texas

Jacque and Sonny Park. They are childhood friends of Sandy's.

～

Hi Art.

Thanks so much for your beautiful words about Sandy, as well as your kind thoughts about Dad. The world gave up two very special people to a better place, and all of us here were blessed to have had them in our lives. I so admired your and Sandy's courage, determi-

nation, fighting spirit, sense of humor, and your great example of unconditional love during your long battle. I am very proud to call both of you friends and family. Let me know if I can ever do anything for you. I look forward to seeing you back on the mountain soon.

All the best,
Randy Banks, Mountain Air, North Carolina

Randy's father, Bill, died the day before Sandy.

Art:

I continue to remember you and Sandy in my prayers. I also have kept all of your e-mails. It is a wonderful love story that continues. I have felt honored to be included in the e-mails. You and Sandy have taught many people a truer and deeper meaning of love and marriage. The courage, spunk and spirit that Sandy exhibited came through in your e-mails.

God bless Sandy and you.

Dick Stansbury, Baltimore, Maryland

Dick is an attorney and friend.

Art,

It is good to have someone to talk to who is going through the same process. The hurt doesn't go away, it just becomes more bearable with time. My cousin moved down here right before Thanksgiving with her husband. They came from California.

We brought them both to Thanksgiving at the Club and they were going up to Lakeland, Florida, to my brother's home for Christmas. He got the flu right before Christmas and then felt better—even played nine holes of golf—and then he died the next day. They had been in Florida for six weeks. We see my cousin a lot now because she is at a loss...it was all so quick. He had been sick, but they said he would live for years longer. I watch her and talk to her and I see how difficult it is—especially as you get older and thought you would spend many happy retirement years together. He was sixty-seven, and they had no retirement time together. You have to keep the memories alive, but you must also live.

Sandy had a wonderful zest for life and she would want you to move forward as you keep her in your heart and soul. You are here and you have many friends, so you should be with them and let them help you through this time. Sometimes you will have to push yourself to move forward and join us, but you have to try. We will be down here through mid-May and would love to get together with you as I am sure many other people would like to do. We have kids and grandkids down here for the next ten days, but if you are here you are welcome to join us for dinner or whatever. Let me know what is going on and I will talk to you soon.

Dottie Lloyd, Naples, Florida

⌒

Dear Art,

I know Sandy is close by you during this difficult time. I just wish we knew more about this whole thing. I played golf for the first time since Sandy died and I felt her presence. Maybe it was because that is how we first met but she was certainly in my thoughts that day and I felt a connection to her. You are in our thoughts and prayers.

Jane and Mike Smith, Naples, Florida

Jane and Mike are our friends from Florida.

∽

Wanted you to know you are in our thoughts. We are home from California and had a good time. We think of you often and of course miss your dear wife, Sandy. She will remain in our hearts forever. You are an inspiration to every woman to have such a loving and caring husband. Hope each day is a little easier for you.

We send much love,

Joel and Kay Levy, Rockport and Houston, Texas

∽

Hi Art,

We have been away and without e-mail access so I am just reading your note today. It is a beautiful note that brought me to tears. Any woman would be fortunate to have been loved in the way you loved Sandy, and the best part is that her love for you was as strong. We will miss her dearly and we will feel fortunate to have known her. She was a unique individual with a tremendous love of life.

We are so glad that we got to spend a little time with her on our visit to Florida. Even then she was concerned about us and didn't speak much of herself. She was gracious to the very end.

Now to you. I do hope that you are doing well (that is, as well as can be expected). The most important thing now is to take care of yourself and especially your own health.

After going through the rollercoaster ride for the past two years, you will need to focus on getting back to a healthy you.

Having gone through the loss of a spouse, I can tell you that the way you feel today will not be how you will feel a year from now, two years from now, and then ten years from now. As hard as it may be to understand, your hurt will lessen over time.

Also, a word of advice. No one—and I mean no one—can or should tell you how long you feel the sadness. You will get on with your life when YOU are ready and not a moment before. You are fortunate that you have many friends and they may try to tell you things to think or do, but just listen to your own head and heart.

When things settle down and you are ready for a break, we would love to have you come and visit us at Dataw. Jim would love to play some golf with you and we can just hang out. Just let us know—the invitation is an open one.

Please keep in touch.

Love,
Dorothy and Jim White, Dataw Island, South Carolina

Dorothy and Jim are our old friends from New York.

~

Thank you so much Arthur. . .we will be thinking of you two tomorrow more than you know. Well, I guess you DO know, you were and are the most special people in the world to us. You were the ones who we wanted more than anything to spend our happiest day together and to come away with us to watch TV (you played shuffleboard!). We will never forget our great times together and we will continue to keep them close to our hearts always. I love Sandy. I miss her terribly. These past few days I had my other sisters visiting me and we reminisced so much about my big sister Sandy and how much I can't bear the thought of never seeing her again. My sister told me I will always see her in my dreams, my heart and in everything I do everyday. She is right, because I do. I hear her voice talking to me, laughing and calling me a little toot. I have so many memories wafting into my thoughts I can't keep track of them all. I look around our house and see all sorts of little Sandy touches everywhere. She had such an impact on my life from the first day I saw her. I know you are fighting a battle every day trying to get to the next. So am I, maybe in a little different way, so are all the people who love her. I see it in the eyes of everyone who mentions her name to me, wishing me a condolence for losing my dearest friend. I am so sorry for our loss! Hope you can find a way to get through this. SO many people love Sandy and you too—for being you, for being her wonderful, loving husband, for taking such good care of her and for always keeping the faith. I wonder when I will stop crying for her. . .it is awful and it hurts so bad. I know you are devastated, but I know you will be strong and continue doing what you do best, being Arthur, the man whom Sandy Benson loved more than anything else in the world.

We love you too. Thank you so much for your anniversary wish for us. Please come and see us when you think you can.

Love,

Maddie and Tony Legner, Rockport, Texas

Sandy thought of Maddie like a kid sister and loved her dearly. Maddie came to see her in February. The reference to "watching TV" was because we went on their honeymoon with them to Port Isabel on South Padre Island, Texas. We didn't think they were really watching TV.

━

So glad you are doing the book. If you need any of your letters you wrote to us while Sandy was with us, let me know. I have kept your e-mails and will treasure them always. Sandy will always be the bright light in your life and we would love to see you in the mountains someday. Boo is a great lady, and I know what a special friendship they must have shared. I will never forget Sandy on our safari trips in high heels, smashing outfits, and fit to kill.

She did her own thing always and carried it off with such style and class. We used to make gestures at each other like "it's you" or something that meant we wanted to make a connection because we had some kind of bond and touched only too little. What a woman!!!

Keep your boogie spirit, keep moving, and don't stop for a minute because Sandy has you under a microscope. You're a kind and loving man who has our respect for, among other things, your crazy ways of expressing yourself and your uncanny sense of humor that tickles the soul.

    Barb and Mo Novikoff, Poway, California

━

Arty:

What can I say to let you know how we are hurting for you. No words. The beauty of Sandy's spirit will always be with you just as she was in the cloud. We are all enriched by having had her in our lives.

You know our thoughts are with you.

I must tell you this story. I saw a dog in the back of a pickup truck the other day and had to laugh about the time Sandy and I went to Dallas to shop when you were building the house in Rockport. We were driving down the freeway in Fort Worth and there was this dog running up and down a piece of plywood that was lying on the bed and up the back of the cab of a pickup that was beside us. Sandy was outraged. She pulled up beside the guy (we were driving 70 miles per hour), rolled down MY window, leaned over and yelled ASSHOLE!!! I thought, "Oh my God, we are going to be shot." Then she sped off, saving us both. I always laugh when I see a dog in a pickup bed, remembering that incident.

Love and prayers.
Glo and Jim Peer, Aransas Pass, Texas

Glo and Jim were childhood friend's of Sandy's.

❧

Art,

Hope you made it home OK. Chugging cold water can really be refreshing after a long cocktail party. We ALL missed Sandy last night, as I felt your sadness and pain across the table, and felt the pain as you went into your private thoughts. Sandy would have laughed as hard as anyone, and somehow I pictured her with us. She is in our hearts, especially as we all return to summer camp. It ain't gonna be a cake walk, but you—and we—will get thru it. You were with only a small part of your Mountain Air family, a unique combination of personalities that blend into a wonderful comfort level that allows us to give and take, and come and go, but, always feeling the love. You're a first class humanoid. OK, I'm going on too long, I'm here for ya when ya need to rant about anything.

Your friend,
MadDog

"Mad Dog" is John Kempfer. He and his wife, Paulette, are friends from the Mountain and Naples.

Arthur and Alan,

*Bob and I are having a little toast to the "birthday girl" tonight.
She lived her life to the fullest, fought a hard battle, found
the loves of her life (Arthur, Alan, Justin, Sophia, and Jack) was
always classy and fashionable. She was smart, witty and totally
charismatic. Enviable in many, many ways. We smile when we
think of her because she was a happy and positive influence in
our lives.*

TO YOU, SANDY!!!!!

Judy and Bob Black, Kingwood, Texas

Judy and Sandy met in New York when they were
hospital roomates delivering their sons on the same
day, May 7, 1969. They remained friends for life.

*Glad to hear you started the book. Often times, as Paul and I
would read your e-mails over the long last year or so, Paul would
remark on your gift with words. You do have that gift, and what
nicer tribute to Sandy than to write about her. I'm sure you'll be
both laughing and weeping but do it with a heart full of her love
of life. What a difference one single life made!*

Take good care of yourself,

Jeanie McGuigan, Knoxville, Tennessee

Jeanie is a dear friend of mine from high school who had
a profound influence on my life. She and her husband,
Paul Norder, live a couple of hours west of the Mountain.

⌒

I know how much you love her, but there are a lot of us who love you, also. We can't take your pain from you, but just know we feel it, too. It'll never pass completely, but with time hopefully it will mellow to a point where you can enjoy both the love of your friends and your memories of Sandy. We lost one part of a great family, don't let us lose the rest for a long time to come. Besides, there's a lot of un-drunk booze out there, and the rest of us can't handle it all without some help from you.

Skip Pierret, Columbus, Indiana

Skip showed up at Sandy's funeral, which was amazing. He said, "I was here at the beginning. I'm here at the end." Skip and I go back to the early 1970s together. He and his wife Stephanie live in Indiana.

⌒

You have had a terrible loss of a wonderful and loving person. That can't get worse, but you have health and lots of friends who care for you a lot and many other things that are blocked by the tragedy that just occurred in your life. You have family, also, and many other blessings that will slowly reappear in your life. As hard as it is, you have to look ahead and live—that is what Sandy would want for you. All she cared about was you and your happiness and one day you will have to be happy again to make her happy!!!

Dottie Lloyd, Naples, Florida

⌒

Arthur,

There has not been a day that has gone by since we left there in February that I have not thought of Sandra, not even a half a day. Linda and I speak of her often and she keeps me up when she has talked to you. I know the times are really hard right now, even a few months will make a difference for your pain to be able to ease some.

You took good care of her for so long and so constantly watched out for her in her illness, and then she had to leave you, even though she is always with you. She knew you and what was going on 'til the end, and she had her mind, which was very important to her. Sandra is a dear friend I knew from the sixth grade when we met at Vacation Bible School at the Baptist Church in Aransas Pass. I thought she was so beautiful in her white blouse and navy skirt. She was always most generous and kind to others who were new, and I treasured my times with her always. We spent the night with slumber parties and went places like the beach or walking to town to the movies, or riding in her Pontiac convertible and posing for pictures in it together. We had some really fun times in those early teen years.

When she first flew from New York back to Aransas Pass to see her parents after she had met and fallen in love with you, I will never forget us going to have coffee together and her telling me about the Champagne and Roses Forever note, which she had with her and about the champagne and roses you had sent her for the limo ride from the airport. None of us know how long our "forever" will be when we are younger and first in love, but we know you had all those wonderful years together and now are writing about them and also the more recent times when cancer robbed you of having more time on earth together. So the title of your book is most suited to what you are going to write of and

we are of course all anticipating your penmanship.
We love and miss Sandra always too.

Sami Shirly, Aransas Pass, Texas

Sami is childhood friend of Sandy's from Aransas Pass. She lost her husband, Troy, to cancer in October, 1989.

⌒

We are glad Sandy is out of pain, but sorry that there wasn't another way. We are so happy the two of you found each other, but sorry you didn't get at least twenty more years. We are grateful that you created so many wonderful memories, but sorry you will be lost in your loss for a while. We hope our friendship will continue to last but will forever miss "our sunshine"!

Judy Black, Kingwood, Texas

A Sign From Sandy

Dear Friends,

Something just happened that's worth relating. I tend not to put stock in things like this, but I'll tell it just the same. I had put a load of laundry in the dryer and I took a glass of wine and went out and sat in the front courtyard, which was among Sandy's and my favorite things to do at the end of the day before dinner. There were some clouds in the sky, but from my vantage point none could be seen. I said aloud, as I've said so many times over the last eighteen days since her passing (eighteen is our lucky number—we met and married on the 18th), "Sandy, please come back to me, in any way you can, please come back to me."

At that moment, a wispy cloud appeared moving left to right. It looked like it could have had a head but not a face, just an oval, and arms. I said, "Sandy is that you? Are you on that cloud?" And then it seemed as if the left arm waved twice and then the cloud just dissipated, then completely disappeared. And now the dog is sticking to me like glue. Who knows? But it made me smile, and I know I'll always remember it.

Art

~

Arthur,

In the "for what it's worth" category, when my dad passed away (and while I was with my mom in Arizona), I was having the same thoughts as you, but not communicating them too much with my mother because of her dementia. One afternoon late, she and I were sitting on their terrace, like we always did, and I was wishing that I would have some "sign" from my father that he was OK. A few moments later, a lone hummingbird came to their feeder. We hadn't seen one in days, maybe weeks, and there it appeared. I chose to believe then and still do that there is some sort of a cosmic/electronic force in our universe that we may not understand but could be real. You know, Arthur, Sandy was always heavenly. I think that was her way of saying, "Hi." She misses you and is hoping you are doing OK. Never give up looking for the "signs"!

Judy Black, Kingwood, Texas

~

It is often said that when someone leaves another behind that soon after they will give a sign that they are watching over them. You have your sign. Sandy will be watching over you as you move on in your life and, knowing Sandy, she will help you through it all. Have faith, keep the memories, and look to what lies ahead. Things always have a way of working out, even when we don't want them to!

Dottie Lloyd, Naples, Florida

~

Dear Art:

Thank you for sharing your incredible moment with us! I have had unexplainable moments in my life in the past and am a great believer. Love does reach beyond the ordinary, beyond science, beyond all of our human accomplishments. I'm so glad you had your Sandy moment and she will always be with you. Take care and keep watching!

Love,

Lauren and Arnie Green, Boca Raton, Florida

~

Art,

That is such a beautiful thought. When we are together soon, I will tell you of the time my father visited me about three months after he passed on. I truly believe those that we love are never, ever, too far away.

Thinking of you,

Paulette Kempfer, Mountain Air and Naples, Florida

Sandy is always there as you just found out. She will not let you go feeling alone. We love her spirit on the cloud. What a woman! She always knew how to fly high, live high, and so like her to just appear on that cloud.

Waving no less. Wave to her for us when you see her again.

Love,
Barb and Mo Novikoff, Poway, California

Arty,

I'll always remember this, too. So glad you shared it with all of us. Sandy IS with you and always will be. I'm so glad she presented herself when you asked. She has such strong energy and it will be with you and us forever.

Linda Lee, Mountain Air, North Carolina

Linda Lee and John Silvati are very dear friends from the Mountain and Cincinnati. They came to Florida every month to see Sandy. Linda was staying with us when Sandy died. Sandy's face always lit up when she saw Linda. They were very, very close.

That is a great story. Believe? Sure, I believe.

Jeanine White, Clarksdale, Mississippi

$\mathcal{P}$ostscript

Art Benson

OCTOBER 2008

As I write this, it's almost eighteen months since I lost Sandy. In the beginning, the pain was almost unbearable. It was actually physical. Now I have some good days and some bad days, but even on the good days there are bad moments. I no longer cry every day, but I still cry for her a lot. I know I should have had time to prepare for her death, but I always believed we could find something, anything, that would save her, or at the very least, buy us more time.

Each passing day draws me one day further away from being with Sandy, but each day also draws me one day closer to being with her always. I'm trying to embrace life as I always have. I have to move on if, for no other reason, it's what Sandy would want me to do, and, as I would have wanted her to do if the positions were reversed. We were both very adaptable, but I haven't quite adapted to this yet. Our fifteen-year-old Whippet, B.B., who was Sandy's favorite because he was a brat, died New Year's Eve, 2007, a fitting end to a horrible year.

In many, many ways she's still with me and always will

be. Sometimes she even makes her presence felt. For example, I had a pair of shorts that Sandy despised, they were beige with black lettering that said "Caveman" on the left leg. They were quite comfortable and I wore them so much the left leg was hanging sort of in a loop. As I was walking through the kitchen on the Mountain in June the hanging loop caught on a drawer pull and whipped me into the granite countertop of the breakfast bar. It slammed my left arm into the rounded countertop edge so hard it punctured my arm and it started bleeding. I have a scar there as a remembrance. I immediately said, "OK, I give up, you win," and changed shorts (once I stopped the bleeding) then threw the "Caveman" shorts away.

There is no question in my mind that Sandy engineered that whole thing. She had a way of always getting what she wanted, and she truly hated those shorts.

In all this time I have only dreamt of Sandy once—at least that I remember. It was June 6, 2007, my beautiful granddaughter Sophia's 4th birthday. In the dream Sandy and I were walking out of what felt like a cave. There was a large rock wall behind us and we were on a beach. It was overcast and the water in front of us felt like the Gulf of Mexico in Port Aransas, Texas. Sandy was stunningly gorgeous and dressed immaculately.

Her hair was up in what I guess is called a French braid. There were no boats on the water and nobody else on the beach. As we walked toward the water I kept telling her over and over, as I always did, that she was the prettiest girl I ever saw in my life and she kept saying, "No, no, no." We were holding hands. As we neared the water she turned to face me and just beamed that spectacular smile of hers. Her back was to the water. Suddenly she was crying and she said, "I don't want to go without you." I said, "It's OK, I just want you to be safe."

That was it. I do hope she's safe. She always loved to sleep, and said that when she slept she wanted it cool and dark and quiet. I would hope she's quite content where she's sleeping now, waiting for me to be by her side once again, but the next time we will never be separated. We will be together for all eternity. The headstone says, "Champagne and Roses Forever." It really was a Champagne and Roses life.

Art Benson

DECEMBER 2009

It's now been almost three years since Sandy died. I still relive some portion of those last days every day. I still talk aloud to her most days, sometimes without realizing I'm doing it, which can lead to some funny situations, like the time I was pumping gas and must have been talking to her because out of the corner of my eye I saw the guy at the next pump slowly backing away. I've still only dreamt of her that one time that I am aware of.

Of course, that dream was vivid enough for a lifetime.

Cleocatra is still with me and doesn't miss the Whippets at all, although I do, but not enough to get another dog. I'm enjoying the lack of responsibility. Had Sandy lived, we would definitely have at least two dogs by now. We owned four acres of commercial land in Sandy's home town of Aransas Pass, Texas, which I sold to the San Patricio County SPCA to build their new headquarters and shelter. At their suggestion, it's being dedicated to, and named for, Sandy. I'm thrilled. It's a fitting tribute to a woman who often said that she thought the wrong species was on top of the food chain.

The kids and grandchildren are a constant source of joy, although I don't see them all that much. Matthew, the oldest, called me two days before Thanksgiving last year (2008) and announced he was getting married the next day. His bride is a beautiful Russian girl named Johanna. A few months ago they went to Russia to meet her family. They got married in a New York State park and held an open cell phone so that I could hear the whole thing. They live in Monroe, New York. Leah got married in September 2008 to Matthew Metzler, who is in Mensa so is obviously very bright, and they live happily in his hometown of Lancaster, Pennsylvania. Alan has remarried a terrific girl named Meredith and they live in Cambridge, Maryland, where they spend a lot of time with Justin, who turned eight years old in January 2010. My son Mark, his wife, Hallie, and their two amazing children (of course they're amazing—all three of my grandchildren are amazing—aren't yours?) live in Golden's Bridge, New York. Mark made all the funeral arrangements when Sandy died, taking a huge burden off me.

The incredible people on the Mountain continue to support and sustain me. I will never be able to adequately express my feelings of gratitude toward them. Eddie and Sarah, who appear earlier in this story, flew me and several other people to New York for the funeral. At the end of my talk in the cemetery, Eddie broke down crying. I didn't expect it and it touched me deeply. It's a moment I'll never forget.

In February of 2008, I moved out of the house in Naples

and into a condo in Bonita Springs, Florida. I simply couldn't stay there any longer. Except for the first seven weeks and the one great party we had in February 2006, nothing good ever happened there. Everywhere I looked something horrible had happened. Moving out has helped. I haven't had to go out socially on my own for a long time and I'm having a hard time with it, although I'm not exactly a shrinking violet. Sandy always managed to know everyone in no time; she just had that kind of personality. As one of the girls on the Mountain, Deb Puckett, said when she first saw Sandy on the golf course, "She's a golfing Barbie." I've dated quite a bit. I'm a very social animal and have met some lovely and fun women. I go back and forth between thinking I'll never get married again to realizing I'm a very coupled person. I like being married. I don't know what the future holds, and I know I can't live in the past, but the past has a strong hold on me. I dated a lovely woman named Patti Wood on and off for some time, but Sandy was a problem for her. It's not that I brought her up a lot, at least I don't think I did, but her presence was there. One night Patti was sleeping in a downstairs bedroom on the Mountain (I had broken my leg slipping on wet grass in June). She said she woke up feeling icy hands on her upper arms. The next day a portrait of the two Whippets hanging over the fireplace in my bedroom came crashing off the wall and shattered. The next day Patti was gone. A couple of months later there were two women visiting at the house. They are cousins (to each other, not to me). One, Pat Odom from Montgomery, Alabama, a former Ms. Senior Alabama, was staying in the large guest room downstairs and the other, Elizabeth Hough, from Flat Rock, Michigan, was staying in the same room and the same bed as the girl was when she felt the "icy fingers." This time Elizabeth said it felt like she was punched in the back and then the next morning the scatter rugs were bunched up and shoved against the wall. She also said she felt like she was punched in the back the next day when she was in the kitchen having a glass of wine. Who knows? I guess stranger things have happened.

One thing is for sure: Sandy was the most profound influence on my life that I could ever have. I loved her then, I love her now, and I will always love her. Together we were magic. Together we were Champagne and Roses.

It's now 2011, almost five years since Sandy's death. On January 3, 2010 I met a stunningly beautiful woman named Maureen Mitchell. We dated a lot and had a great time. For the first time since I lost Sandy, I had deep feelings for someone. Maureen went to the Mountain with me in May, and I was amazed at the depth of what I felt, but perhaps I subconsciously felt guilty and I pretty much messed up the whole thing and Maureen went home on September 22. She said she would come back, and I kept hoping she would, but it was not to be. Lately we've seen each other socially and remain friends. Maureen is an extraordinary woman and it was from her that I learned that I could actually have very deep feelings for someone again. In spite of the words of the dedication of the book—"*For Sandy, who taught me how to love and because of her I can love again*"— I never really believed the second part; although I wrote it, it was more wishful thinking than anything else. I think I'm finally coming out of it though. I'm going to sell the car I bought for Sandy a month before she was diagnosed. I've put the condo on the market and will move to Naples, closer to my Mountain friends who live there, and closer to a much more active social scene. Contrary to the saying "Time heals all wounds," it doesn't. It just makes things a bit easier to accept. It still feels like just yesterday that I lost her, though. Today, as we've done every year since we first came to Florida in 2005, I'm going to Mort and Boo Mortenson's for Thanksgiving with their family and friends. I was fortunate enough to get three invitations, all from dear friends, but Mort and Boo always ask first, and it's always a great time. We met them on the Around the World trip in 2003.

It's now the seventh Thanksgiving since we first came to Florida, and my fifth without Sandy. I guess it's easier now, but I still talk aloud to her almost every day. I still can't hold back the tears sometimes, and I don't always know what sets it off, although every time I have to re-read this book, as I recently did for the second edition, I come apart at the seams, particularly the parts leading up to, and following, Sandy's death. Most of the comments I've gotten are quite similar: "I passed it along to friends battling Cancer". . . "I laughed and I cried and I laughed and I cried" . . . and, particularly from women who never met her, "I only wish I could have known her." On June 11, 1990 I wrote a poem to my sons that Sandy loved and, as such, I don't think it's inappropriate to include it here in her story.

> To My Sons

> 1.
> *I once was a young man exactly like you,*
> *With hopes and dreams I thought would come true*
> *Nothing would ever stand in my way*
> *I thought time would stand still, each day was my day.*

2.
Little by little my future was past.
It dawned on me slowly, my youth wouldn't last.
But even today, though it's no more than a dream,
I sometimes feel I can do what I did at eighteen.

3.
The clock keeps its steady march to the right:
As night follows day, so day follows night.
Then suddenly, before I even gave it a thought,
The years have rushed by and time has grown short.

4.
How swiftly the circle, which once seemed so wide,
Shrinks smaller around me, it can't be denied.
So for you who will someday stand in my place,
Taste life to the fullest but live it with grace.

5.
Just bear it in mind when you see someone old,
Whose time has long passed, whose dreams have
    turned cold,
That their hearts were once young, their passions
    were strong,
they laughed and they loved and it could never go wrong.

6.
Someday when you see young men running at play,
You'll stop and you'll think, and you might want
  to say,
"It's hard to believe but it really is true.
I once was a young man exactly like you."

Matthew Benson

DECEMBER 2009

It's hard to believe it is nearly three years since Sandy died. Sandy made a big impact in the life of my father, Arthur Benson, as well myself and my siblings. There was a pizzazz about Sandy and this is a word that doesn't often come to mind when you think of someone. She was a determined and driven individual. A southern Texas lady with Cherokee Indian in her bloodline and enough years of living in New York to gain that "New Yorker" sensibility as well. She spoke her mind, regardless of if you agreed or not. Several times, I did not. No matter, though, because honestly, who agrees with everyone all the time? I know that the quality of life she shared with my father—the life journeys they had, the friends they made, the places they went, the songs they sang, the jokes they told—these things that worked between the two of them are exactly what all people would like to experience in their own lives. Sandra was the catalyst of that.

Sandra Benson was technically my stepmother. The last time I saw Sandy—in February of 2007—I told her something which had only recently occurred to me.

Through twenty years, Sandy never introduced me to anyone as "my stepson Matthew." The same with my brother, Mark, and sister, Leah. Sandy's son, Alan, from her first marriage was our brother, not stepbrother. She called me her son, as with Mark and Leah (Leah, obviously, was "daughter"). There was no extra term or word that she used, but simply son or daughter. I guess when you grow up in a divorce scenario, these terms are standard, almost "go-to" terminology. I told Sandy the last time I saw her that I recognized and always would appreciate this. I could tell it meant a lot to her for me to acknowledge the relevance and importance of this. Sandra was not my "step" mother. She was a mother in my life, much like I was a son in her life—or we were the children in her life.

Mark C. Benson

DECEMBER 2009

There are some things I always found particularly interesting about Sandy. First, she was the only person I've ever heard of who got a scholarship to college (University of Miami) for baton twirling. Honestly, has anyone ever heard of this? Second, at any given sporting event you could expect to see and hear Sandy going over the top with her excitement for whichever team she was cheering for. Literally jumping up and down, clutching the person next to her and shaking them vigorously, be it a stranger or one of us, and whooping and hollering like a person who's just found out they won the lottery when her team did something good. Her son, Alan, is very much the same way in that regard, and when the two of them were together it was truly hysterical. Third, she definitely enjoyed to enjoy. She truly had a zest for the things in life that she held dear, and it was a rare occasion that I saw her get down in the dumps over something, or upset about the laundry list of things that can upset or frustrate most of us on a daily basis. She and dad lived a charmed life and were deeply, madly in love. It was a palpable feeling whenever I was around the two of them together. When she got sick she kept her head up and her attitude was inspiring. I know that almost 'til the end she believed she would persevere, and it seems to me that only when Sandy decided it was time, did she allow the disease to take her.

Dad kept an incredible attitude throughout as well. He was a machine, making sure she got all her pills and did all the things that she was supposed to, including feeding her vitamin shakes and trying to keep her as active as possible. They would whisk from one doctor to another specialist, to an herbalist, researching new alternative medications and so on. I don't know how he did it for so long, but I guess you do what you have to most willingly when you're fighting for your life, or the life of your dearest loved one. I do know that dad seemed to me to be unable to see the physical changes that Sandy was going through. I think when he looked at Sandy he always saw her as she looked before she got sick.

One of the last times I saw Sandy she was barely able to speak because every breath was a struggle. I asked her if she was ready to go, and she smiled and nodded that she was. It was an overwhelming feeling leaving the house to return to the airport that day because although we didn't spend a lot of time together since she and dad moved away from New York, I knew I would never see her again. It was a very sad feeling, I'll remember it vividly the rest of my life. I'll also always remember the few days after the funeral when dad stayed with my family. He would let out these enormous sighs, as if he had forgotten to breathe for a few minutes. He told me that his hurt was more than just emotional, that what he was feeling was a physical pain. Watching him those few days, I know for a fact that what he said was true. Sandy was the one for dad and dad the one for Sandy.

Leah Benson Metzler

DECEMBER 2009

When I was younger, Sandy told me that she was twenty-one years old, which I had no problem believing. However, I started to get a little suspicious when her son, Alan, was nineteen. As ridiculous as it is, what finally gave it away was Sandy telling someone she had her ears pierced when she was forty. I think I believed it for so long because, first of all, my dad would *never* lie to me, and second of all, Sandy was so energetic and vivacious, she really could have been mistaken for a twenty-one-year-old. She was a beautiful woman with impeccable taste. (Hey, she picked my dad, right?) There have been so many times when I have wanted to call her and ask her opinion on something, so truly not a day goes by when I don't think about her.

What I found so amazing throughout her struggle, with the exception of the last few months, was that she never allowed herself to be sick. She went about her regular life enjoying every day and didn't sit at home feeling sorry for herself. Sandy will always be a huge part of my dad's life (and our lives), as she should be, and it's really hard to think that she is no longer here. When I call my dad, I still half-expect her to pick up and say, "Hey girl!" I can still actually hear her saying that. Everybody should be so lucky to experience a love that is a fraction as deep as theirs was. You can feel it in the pages of this book. There was honestly nothing my dad wouldn't have done to save her and I think every day she lived was a gift. I think because of this book, her spirit will live forever and hopefully inspire others to embrace every day as fully as she did.

Alan Girard

DECEMBER 2009

My mother looks out at me from the mantle above our fireplace. She sparkles in a sunny summer dress, ready for the big day. A vintage Pontiac gleams by her side, but it doesn't get my attention. She is the star. Her hand delicately brushes the chrome curving along the driver's side door. A stockingless foot, trim and petite, in summer pumps angles forward on the hot pavement, its heel tucked neatly inside the arch of the other. Even from across the room she catches my eye. The shimmering radiance of my mother's elegance and grace are impossible to miss.

She was a teenager then, about the same age I was when I started to get to know her. Her daddy ran a dealership in her hometown and he likely had something to do with the car. It might have been her first, but I don't know for sure if it was. There were lots of things I didn't know about mom then. Like that for a long time she used to spend most of the day alone in bed after getting me off to school in the morning. Or that she secretly nipped at a gallon of wine she kept in the trunk of her car when she was out. You needed those things to get along with my father. You needed something just to get you by.

Mom would sit me down every so often while I was growing up and tell me things with dad weren't going well. Some changes needed to be made, she would say. Then she would move into the guest bedroom or get an apartment, only to come back later and try to work things out. She never said as much, but I think she stuck around so long to keep from breaking up our family. She really wanted to make things work for herself, of course, but I think she also wanted to avoid letting down her only son.

Eventually, though, mom moved out for good. She met Arthur and everything changed. He was the best thing that ever happened to her. You could tell they were meant to be together. He adored how my mother's beauty seemed to shine from within. She was enchanted by his generous spirit and big heart. Arthur's infectious humor literally breathed new life into mom, and she would later say the secret to a good marriage is to laugh often. Over the years, hundreds of people would be inspired by the magic of Sandy and Arthur.

After college, I eventually settled down and started a family of my own. Justin is named after my mom's dad, and now he is already well on his way to becoming a lovely young man. Like mom's first marriage, my first marriage ended, although it did when Justin was at a much younger age than I was when my parents went their separate ways.

Also, like mom's second marriage, my second marriage is more than I could ever hope for. Meredith and I celebrate two years together this month, but it feels like we have been together for a very long time.

Not long after Meredith and I met, mom and I were Christmas shopping for Justin. I was steadying myself for my first holiday season as a single parent, and was getting overwhelmed with the idea that divorce is a broken promise made to children who rightfully expect to be raised by two loving parents under one roof. It's a source of guilt I still struggle with today. I think mom struggled with it too.

Even though the year I was divorced was hard for me, it was one during which I felt closer to my mother than ever before. We had kept in touch over the years after college, but rarely did we talk about matters of the heart. It wasn't until I began sharing feelings with her about my divorce that I felt like she was really there for me. We were on the phone regularly, and the more I talked, the more she listened and offered words of wisdom and support.

So it was that morning after Christmas shopping that her reaction to my upwelling of feelings of failure as a father was such a surprise. She listened as she had before, but suddenly, she became quiet and withdrawn. A veil had lowered and I knew that our conversation would soon be over.

In that moment, despite being so self-occupied, I felt as if I was beginning to understand something essential about my mother. Anyone who has seen Sandy perform "Hotel California" on karaoke night knows she had an intense passion for life. It's what captivated and inspired so many of those who knew and loved her, my father included. But when mom and dad were together, she could not let her inner beauty shine, using all of her energy instead just to hold on.

Later, it seemed as if this dark time in our lives still stuck with her. Long after she left my father, mom was still sometimes reserved toward me, as if the remorse she might have had over our broken family was still alive. The day she saw me suffering over what I thought of as a failed parenthood, I imagined her remembering her own grief over being less than a mother than she had wanted to be. I thought I saw regret in her the same way I had felt regret in myself. That's when I knew for sure that even though sometimes she seemed withdrawn, she didn't love me any less. She was just reacting to feelings of her own.

Mom died the following spring. She was buried on a hillside that I had been by hundreds of times as a child. The memories I have of that time in my life are faded now, good thoughts and bad mingled in a past I don't think much about anymore. Going by that hillside today, I have no regrets. I think of mom and am thankful for her zest for life, a trait that enriched many and one that I'm proud to carry forward.

If mom did feel remorse for not having been all she wanted to be, I understand and accept it. And I forgive her. Like the rest of us, I know she only did the best she could possibly do. And if my current and "final" marriage (as mom and Arthur liked to say of their own) is any indication, mom raised a son who couldn't be more happy and successful in life. I thank her for that too.

Earlier this year, Meredith and I went through some old slides my dad had given me. She framed the image that now hangs over our fireplace. In my mind, my mother is still as radiant as she was when that photo was taken. From her perch there on the mantle, she watches over me and my family, and she is pleased with what her son has become.